Positively Vegetarian

by

Rachel Demuth

Demuths Restaurant

chupi publishing

First published in 1997 by
Chupi Publishing
2 North Parade Passage
BATH BA1 1NX

The information in this book was correct to the best of the author's & publisher's
belief at the time of going to press. While no responsibility can be accepted for
errors and omissions, the author and publisher would welcome corrections and
suggestions for material to include in subsequent editions of this book.
So get writing.

The moral right of the author has been asserted.

Design & cover photographs by Nicho Troup

Illustrations by Claudio Muñoz

Printed & bound in Great Britain by
The Bath Press, Bath, England

ISBN 0 9531119 0 3

CONTENTS

INTRODUCTION

This first Demuths cookbook is the result of countless
requests for recipes from our restaurant customers.
Many times over the years I have been asked by them,
'How did you make that?', and so many times I've scribbled
the recipe down with instructions for them to scale it down
and use their imagination as to the method and the
ingredients.
A handful of this ..... a splash of that .....
These rushed affairs have gone all over the world.
I often receive messages of thanks and a special recipe of
theirs to try out in the restaurant.

I've never felt precious or secretive about our recipes.
Sharing recipes is an exciting way of discovering about other
cultures, different ways of doing the same task or unusual
flavour combinations.
As with all recipes, they come from somewhere, are handed
from one person to another and are fine tuned and passed
onwards.
Recipes that have been passed down through generations
now criss-cross the world.
Some may be unique, but most come about through adapting
recipes to ingredients that you have in your kitchen.
Some combinations turn out to be fantastic and others
inedible.
That's the joy of cooking.

I hope that this collection of recipes can be a starting point
for you to gain inspiration. Adapt them if you wish and
create your own versions.
If they work for you, or those who eat them, pass them on.
Whatever you do, enjoy them and make them with love.

Rachel

THANKS

This collection of recipes has had contributions from cooks from all over world and over many years.

Thanks firstly to the team who made this book possible:

Wanda Nowak who was the creative force in producing these recipes as well as cooking for the immediacy of thousands of hungry customers.

Guy Foster for his cosmically perfect salads and unstinting labours.

Mark Banbury for his stunning dishes, his ability to settle for nothing less than perfection, and for being able to cope with a ceaseless queue of punters on Saturdays.

Emma Moffat for keeping the customers obliviously unaware of the madness behind the scenes.

Troy Griffin for being the only one of us with the bottle to wear a tie and a waistcoat.

Marie Morley for proofing, correcting our numerous mistakes and cracking unmentionable jokes to lighten our evenings.

Katie Hardman for her recipe testing and vegan contributions.

Esther Smith for her far out cooking and testing of recipes.

Lisa Sullivan for her middle eastern contribution.

Allesandro Stella for his Italian wildness.

Liz Bullen for her ace cooking and big smile.

Jo Crockett for her chocolate fudge cake and for managing Demuths and us for over 2 years.

Claudio Muñoz for his illustrations.

My partner Nicho for his positivity and general madness.

And thanks to all our customers, past, present and future whose appreciation makes it all worth while and whose continued custom makes our endeavours possible.

NOTES ON INGREDIENTS

In vegetarian cooking, you will need some specialist ingredients and vegetarian alternatives to standard ingredients.

APPLE JUICE CONCENTRATE
Apple juice concentrate is an excellent substitute for sugar and can be used to sweeten both sweet and savoury dishes.
For vegans, use apple juice concentrate instead of honey.

CHEESE
Vegetarian cheese is made with a non-animal, microbial rennet used to curdle the milk, rather than the traditional animal rennet from the lining of a calves stomach.
On packaged cheeses look out for the V symbol.

COUSCOUS
It is the traditional staple grain in North Africa and is made by steaming, drying and cracking grains of duram wheat.
It can be used as a substitute for rice.

CREAMED COCONUT AND COCONUT MILK
Creamed coconut is made from the compressed white flesh of the coconut.
Coconut milk is also made from the white flesh of the coconut, but rather than compressing it into a block it is diluted to a cream like consistency and tinned.
Use creamed coconut and coconut milk as a vegan alternative to dairy cream in curries and oriental dishes.

EGGS
The recipes are scaled for size 3 eggs and free-range are best.

FAT
Use salted butter for savoury dishes and unsalted for sweet dishes.
When margarine is required use pure sunflower or soya margarine.
Make sure that the margarine you choose is suitable for vegetarians. Some brands contain fish oil.
If catering for vegans, make sure that there is no added whey in it.

FILO PASTRY AND PUFF PASTRY
Filo pastry and puff pastry are best bought frozen because they are so time consuming to make.

FLOUR
If possible buy organic flour.
For brown, the best is 100% stoneground wholewheat.
For white, choose unbleached white.
Gram Flour is used in Indian cooking.
It is milled from pulses, most commonly chickpeas and is also gluten free.

HERBS
Use fresh where ever possible.
All the recipes use fresh herbs but if you only have dried ones
1teaspoon of dried herbs =1tablespoon of fresh herbs.

LEMONGRASS
It's best fresh and looks like dried grass with a fleshy stem.
It has a distinctive aroma and a sweet and sour citrus flavour.
Add the whole stem at the beginning of cooking and its flavour will
infuse into the dish but remember to take it out before serving.

NORI SEAWEED
Nori is the most commonly used Japanese seaweed.
It is traditionally used for the outer shell of sushi .
If making sushi (nori rolls), buy ready toasted nori.
If you can't get toasted nori, you can try toasting it over a gas flame.
Untoasted nori is very tough and chewy to eat.

OILS
Sunflower oil has a neutral flavour and is ideal for everyday use and
can be used for savoury, sweet dishes and frying, as well as dressings.
Toasted Sesame oil has a nutty taste and imparts an oriental flavour to
dishes.
Olive oil is graded according to its acidity.
The lower the acidity the better the oil.
The purest is extra virgin which is also the darkest in colour and the
strongest in flavour. Use it for salad dressings.
The next best is virgin olive oil which is lighter in colour and flavour
and and can be used for cooking or dressings.
As walnut and hazelnut oil are very expensive, you can add a
teaspoon to sunflower oil to pep up a salad dressing.

POLENTA
Polenta is the essential staple ingredient of northern Italy and is made
from yellow maize flour.
It is golden in colour and gluten free.
Try and buy 'quick cook' polenta flour as it is much easier to make into
polenta because it needs less stirring.

PULSES
Dried beans, peas and lentils are known as pulses.
Except for lentils and split peas, most pulses need to be soaked before
cooking.
Place them in a large bowl and cover with three times their volume of
water.
Soak them for about 8 hours, rinse well, pick out any small stones and
then cook them in plenty of fresh water until they are tender.

RICE

As a staple, use a long grain brown rice, preferably organic.
For oriental dishes, white basmati rice and fragrant Thai rice are lighter and have a more subtle flavour.
For a risotto, arborio rice is essential as it has a plump grain and more starch than other rice.
As the arborio rice cooks, the starch is released and this gives the risotto its creamy consistency.
Wild rice is not a true rice but a grass seed grown in the Great Lakes area of North America. It is shining black in colour and nutty in texture and takes twice as long to cook as brown rice.

SALT and PEPPER

Sea salt is the best type of salt to use, for its purity, trace elements and flavour.
Freshly ground black pepper is preferable to powdered pepper for its freshness.
As an alternative to black peppercorns, try a four peppercorn mix of white, black, green and pink, freshly ground for a milder aromatic taste.

SEASONINGS

For stock, we prefer bouillon powder to stock cubes. Bouillon powder has a more delicate flavour, is easier to measure out and can be dissolved directly into the dish.
Choose one that is lactose free and low in salt.
Yeast extract, Vitam-R, Marmite or Vecon are useful for adding colour and flavour to stews and gravies.
The flavour can be overpowering so use sparingly.

SEITAN

Seitan is wheat gluten. It is vegan and high in protein and is traditionally used as a meat substitute in Chinese cooking. It is often known as 'mock duck'.
It can be chopped or sliced and added to stews or stir frys to provide texture, flavour and protein. It sometimes comes marinaded in tamari.

SHOYU AND TAMARI

Shoyu and tamari are naturally fermented japanese soya sauces used to enhance the flavour of savoury dishes.
Shoyu is made from soya beans, wheat, salt and water.
Tamari is made from soya beans, salt and water, is more concentrated than shoyu and is gluten free.
All the recipes use shoyu, but if you are cooking for someone who is allergic to gluten, use tamari and halve the quantities.
When buying shoyu or tamari, buy from a wholefood shop or if buying from a supermarket, check the ingredients because some commercially produced soya sauces contain caramel and artificial flavourings.

SOYA MILK AND SOYA CREAM

Soya milk is made from soya beans and is vegan and gluten free.
It is high in protein, low in fat and free from cholesterol.
In cooking, soya milk can be used as substitute for cows milk in soups, sauces, quiches, puddings and milkshakes.
Soya cream is a wonderful new product and can be used as a vegan substitute for dairy cream.

THAI CURRY PASTE

Thai curry paste is an essential ingredient for an authentic Thai curry.
Make sure that it is vegetarian as some brands contain fish paste.

TOFU

Tofu is soya bean curd.
It is made from soya milk in a process similar to cheese making and has been a staple food in the East for thousands of years.
It is vegan and gluten free and is an invaluable source of protein for those on a vegan diet.
Tofu is very nutritious.
It is high in protein, iron, calcium and B vitamins but low in fat and free from cholesterol.
It is very versatile and because it has a bland flavour, it can soak up what ever flavours you want.
It can be used in savoury or sweet dishes, pureed for a dip, cubed and marinated for kebabs, blended and sweetened for a cheesecake.
Tofu can be used as a substitute for eggs, as it sets when cooked.
Use it for quiches and baked cheesecakes.
As well as plain tofu, smoked and marinated tofu are widely available.
Tofu must be refrigerated and stored covered with water.

TOMATOES, SUN DRIED

Buy packed sun dried tomatoes and not those in oil.
Soak them in boiling water for at least ½ hour until they are rehydrated, then drain.
Marinate in extra virgin olive oil.

VINEGARS

Balsamic Vinegar is the most expensive and revered vinegar.
It traditionally comes from Modena in Northern Italy and is made from the juice of sweet Trebbiano grapes and then aged in wooden barrels.
It has a slightly sweet, tangy taste and a rich dark colour.
Wine vinegars, red or white are good staple vinegars for salad dressings, as they go well with olive oil and in Mediterranean dishes.
Cider vinegar has a rougher taste than wine vinegar and is best suited to cold climate dishes such as spicy red cabbage.
Malt vinegar is so strongly flavoured and pungent that it is best used only for pickling.
Rice vinegar is very subtle and is used in Oriental cooking.

UTENSILS and EQUIPMENT NEEDED

Vegetarian cooking does not require any specialised utensils or kitchen equipment but for this recipe book there is some equipment that you will need which is mostly labour saving.

FOOD PROCESSOR
A food processor is the number one labour saving device and is invaluable for making pâté, mixing pastry, blending soups, beating egg whites, chopping, grinding and grating. Most of our recipes make use of a food processor.

BLENDER
An electric blender is useful for making smooth soups, sauces and mayonnaise. A blender purées to a much smoother consistency than is achievable with a food processor.

ELECTRIC HAND WHISK
An electric hand whisk is useful for small tasks such as beating egg whites, mixing batters and whipping cream.

WOK
A Wok is a Chinese frying pan, rounded in shape, made of thin metal and designed for quick stir frying.
They are traditionally made of carbon iron and need regular oiling to stop them rusting.
For home use, a stainless steel wok is preferable as it is maintenance free.
Woks are designed to balance on a stand over a flame.
If you do not have a gas cooker, flat bottomed woks are available for electric cookers.

HEAVY BOTTOMED SAUCEPAN
A heavy bottomed pan is useful for slow cooking, 'le Creuset' enamelled saucepans are ideal as they have the added advantage of being oven proof.

SET OF MEASURING SPOONS
Essential for accurate measuring.
1 teaspoon=5 mls
1 tablespoon=15 mls

All the recipes have been scaled down to manageable sizes,
and are of ample portions.

MEASUREMENT CONVERSION TABLES

All of these conversions are approximate.
All of the weights & measures in the recipes are metric.

WEIGHT

GRAMMES TO OUNCES

8gms	¼oz
15gms	½oz
20gms	¾oz
25gms	1oz
50gms	2oz
75gms	3oz
100gms	4oz
150gms	5oz
175gms	6oz
200gms	7oz
225gms	8oz
250gms	9oz
275gms	10oz
300gms	11oz
350gms	12oz
375gms	13oz
400gms	14oz
425gms	15oz
450gms	16oz
1 Kilo	2lbs 3oz

FLUID

MILLILITRES TO FLUID OUNCES TO PINTS

25ml	1 fl oz
50ml	2 fl oz
75ml	3 fl oz
100ml	4 fl oz
150ml	5 fl oz
275ml	½ pint
425ml	¾ pint
570ml	1 pint
1 litre	1¾ pint
1150ml	2 pint

TEMPERATURE

HEAT SETTINGS

110°c	225°F	GAS ¼
130°c	250°F	GAS ½
140°c	275°F	GAS 1
150°c	300°F	GAS 2
170°c	325°F	GAS 3
180°c	350°F	GAS 4
190°c	375°F	GAS 5
200°c	400°F	GAS 6
220°c	425°F	GAS 7
230°c	450°F	GAS 8
240°c	475°F	GAS 9

Starters

Olive, Chickpea and Aubergine Tapenade

A chunky, garlicky tapenade. Delicious spread on wholewheat toast.

Serves 6

3 large aubergines

6 tablespoons olive oil

125gms chickpeas, dried weight

150gms black olives, pitted

2 garlic cloves, finely chopped

1 tablespoon lemon juice

2 tablespoons parsley, chopped

2 tablespoons red peppers, finely diced

sea salt and freshly ground black pepper

Soak the chickpeas overnight and then cook them in plenty of fresh water until tender.
Preheat oven to 220C/Gas7/425F.
Prick the aubergines all over and put into the preheated oven for about 45 minutes or until the aubergines feel soft and look wrinkled.
Leave the aubergines to cool, then peel and discard the skins. Chop them roughly and put them into a food processor along with the drained, cooked chickpeas, garlic, lemon juice and olive oil.
Purée until smooth, adding water if the mixture is too stiff.
Add the black olives, parsley and finely chopped red pepper and blend again for a few seconds, retaining the chunky texture. Season to taste.
Chill before serving, spread on wholewheat toast.

Bombay Potatoes

These yellow spiced potatoes can either be served as a starter with chutney or as an accompaniment to a vegetable curry.

Serves 6

6 medium potatoes, scrubbed, not peeled

75ml sunflower oil

1 onion, thinly sliced

2 garlic cloves, peeled and chopped

1 teaspoon turmeric

1 pinch sea salt

½ teaspoon chilli powder

1 teaspoon ground cumin

1 teaspoon black mustard seed

Cook the whole unpeeled potatoes in boiling water until just tender.
Drain and leave them to cool.
Sauté the chopped onion and garlic in sunflower oil until golden.
Add the spices, stir well and cook until the mustard seeds begin to pop.
Be careful not to burn the spices.
Cut the potatoes into bite sized pieces and pour the oil and spice mixture over them.
Leave for a few hours to let the spices soak into the potatoes.
Serve warm with mango chutney.

Brie and Cranberry Scrunchies

The cranberry filling gives these filo parcels a festive touch. You will need a patty(bun) tin with 12 indentations.

Makes 12 scrunchies

9 sheets filo pastry

175gms brie cheese

12 teaspoons cranberry sauce

25gms melted butter

Preheat the oven to 220C/Gas7/425F.
Cut the brie into 12 equal sized squares.
Detach 9 sheets of filo pastry from the roll, wrap up the remaining filo and return it to the fridge.
Place the 9 sheets on top of one another on a clean surface and cut into 4 equal squares.
Cover with a damp cloth to prevent the filo drying out and crumbling.
Take 3 squares at a time.
Brush each square with melted butter and lay them overlapping each other to form a 12 pointed star shape.
Gently press the star shape into the greased bun tin.
Place a square of brie and a teaspoon of cranberry sauce in the middle of the filo.
Draw up the edges of the filo into the centre and scrunch together.
Repeat this process until you have filled your bun tin.
Brush each scrunchy with melted butter and bake in the preheated oven for approx 10minutes until golden brown.

Cream Cheese, Mint and Apricot Dip

This dip must be made with fresh mint. It is very easy to make, deliciously rich and best served with warm naan bread.

Serves 4

50gms dried apricots

250gms low fat cream cheese

½ tablespoon chopped fresh mint

½ garlic clove, peeled

fresh mint leaves for decoration

Soak the apricots in boiling water for about 20 minutes or until they are plump.
Discard the water and put the apricots in a food processor along with the garlic and chopped fresh mint.
Blend the mixture until nearly smooth but with little chunks of apricot remaining to give the dip a chunky texture.
Add the cream cheese and blend again.
If the dip is too thick add a little milk.
Chill before serving.
Decorate with mint leaves.

Baba Ganoush

A delicious creamy aubergine dip with a mild smoky flavour.
Serve with toasted pitta bread.

Serves 6

6 whole aubergines

1½ tablespoons lemon juice

6 cloves garlic, peeled

3 tablespoon shoyu

3 tablespoon tahini

freshly ground black pepper

Split the aubergines in half and roast them in a hot oven until
the skins are wrinkled and the flesh is cooked.
Remove from the oven and allow to cool.
Remove the insides of the aubergines and place in a food
processor.
Add the lemon juice, garlic, shoyu and tahini.
Blend until smooth.
Add freshly ground black pepper to taste.
Chill before serving with toasted pitta bread.

Curried Cheese Fondue

This fondue is very rich and ideally served in a specialised fondue kit. If you don't have one, use a flame proof casserole dish that can be returned to a heat source when it cools down.

Serves 4

200ml cider

3 tablespoons sherry

225gms cheddar cheese, grated

110gms edam, grated

1 tablespoon soft brown sugar

1 teaspoon madras curry powder

2 teaspoons shoyu

1 teaspoon mustard powder

½ teaspoon cornflour

Put the cider in a double boiler or a thick bottomed saucepan and bring the cider to the boil.
Add the sugar and the curry powder.
Stir continuously until the sugar has melted.
Add the shoyu and mustard powder and stir well.
Add both the cheddar cheese and edam cheese and continue to stir until the cheeses have melted.
Remove the saucepan from the heat and stir in the sherry.
Season to taste.
Mix the cornflour with a little cold water to a smooth paste and stir into the cheese mixture.
Return to the heat and stir until the cornflour has thickened the fondue.
Serve hot and bubbling with chunks of bread to dunk into the fondue.

Guacamole Dip

This is a very creamy smooth avocado dip to serve with tortilla chips or as an accompaniment to nachos.

Serves 6

3 large avocados

3 garlic cloves, peeled

½ red chilli, de-seeded

100ml sunflower oil

3 tablespoons lemon juice

pinch of sea salt

In a food processor purée the peeled garlic and the de-seeded chilli with half the sunflower oil.
Peel and remove the stones from the avocados and roughly chop.
Place the chopped avocados in the food processor with the pureed garlic and chilli and blend again, slowly adding the remaining sunflower oil.
Finally add the lemon juice and sea salt and blend again.
Chill before serving.

Hummus

This recipe for hummus is nutty, garlicky and has a strong olive oil flavour, so different from the bland creamy versions that you can buy.

Serves 8

250gms chickpeas, dry weight

or

2 x 425gm tins of chickpeas

6 garlic cloves, peeled

150ml olive oil

2 lemons, juiced

3 tablespoons tahini

225ml water

sea salt and freshly ground black pepper

You need cooked chickpeas for this recipe.
If you are using dried chickpeas soak them overnight and cook them in lots of fresh water until tender.
If you are using tinned chickpeas, make sure that they are sugar free and that they are drained and rinsed before you use them.
In the food processor, puree the peeled garlic cloves, the drained cooked or tinned chickpeas, olive oil, lemon juice and tahini to a thick paste.
Then add the water slowly and purée until the hummus is the required consistency - runny for a dip and stiffer for a spread.
Season with sea salt and freshly ground black pepper to taste.
Chill before serving.
Serve with warm pitta bread.

Creamy Broccoli and Stilton Ramekins

A very quick and easy starter to make.
You'll need 6 individual ramekin dishes.

Serves 6

1 head of broccoli

150gms Stilton cheese

20gms butter

20gms unbleached white flour

220ml single cream

110ml milk

pinch of sea salt

pinch of paprika

Divide the broccoli into small florets and plunge into a pan of boiling water.
Simmer for a few minutes until the broccoli is just tender.
Then strain the broccoli and plunge it into cold water.
The cold water will arrest the cooking process and bring the broccoli back to a bright green colour.
Divide the broccoli into the ramekins.
Crumble the Stilton over the broccoli.
Melt the butter over a medium heat in a small saucepan.
Remove from the heat and stir in the flour.
Put back onto the heat and slowly stir in the cream and milk to make a smooth white sauce.
Season to taste.
Pour the white sauce over the broccoli and sprinkle with paprika.
Place under a hot grill until the sauce begins to bubble and turn golden.
Serve at once with warm ciabatta bread.

Nori Rolls with Orange and Toasted Sesame Sauce

These nori rolls are very easy to make. Ensure that you buy sushi nori seaweed that has already been toasted over a flame.

Serves 6

Rolls

150gms white basmati rice (unrinsed)

¼ teaspoon turmeric

425ml water

1 small red pepper, very finely diced

30gms sultanas

2 heaped teaspoons blue poppy seeds

3 sheets of sushi nori seaweed

Sauce

1 orange, juiced

2 teaspoons shoyu

1 tablespoon toasted sesame oil

1 piece of fresh ginger root

Do not rinse the rice before cooking.
Put the rice, turmeric and water into a saucepan with a well fitting lid.
Boil the rice with the lid on, until it is almost cooked.
Turn off the heat and leave it to stand with the lid on.
(This will allow the rice to absorb all the remaining water)
Whilst the rice is cooling, make the sauce.

Orange & Toasted Sesame Sauce

Mix the freshly squeezed orange juice with the shoyu and the toasted sesame oil.
Grate the ginger root with its skin on, into a separate bowl.
Take the grated pieces of ginger into the palm of your hand and squeeze to extract the ginger juice.
Add this to the orange juice, shoyu and sesame oil.
Mix it well.

Nori Rolls

Add the finely diced red pepper, the sultanas and the poppy seeds to the rice and mix well.
Lay out the nori sheets individually on a work surface.
Divide the rice mixture equally between them.
Spread the mixture evenly over the surface of the nori sheets, leaving a 2cm strip uncovered on the edge of each sheet.
Moisten the edges with water.
Roll up the nori rolls like a Swiss roll.
Stick them together along the moistened edge leaving them to rest with the join facing downwards.
To serve, slice each nori roll into six with a very sharp non-serrated knife.
Place three rounds on each plate and drizzle the sauce over them.

Penne Rigate in a Cream, Tomato and Fresh Basil Sauce

This pasta dish is best made with sweet late summer tomatoes and a copious quantity of fresh basil.

Serves 4

100gms penne rigate pasta

275ml double cream

5 ripe, sweet tomatoes, diced

2 tablespoons fresh basil, chopped

sea salt and freshly ground black pepper

Bring a large pan of salted water to the boil and cook the pasta until a denté.
Rinse the cooked pasta in cold water, drain well and put into a large mixing bowl.
Add the cream and chopped basil to the pasta and stir well.
Dice the tomatoes finely and stir into the pasta mixture.
Season to taste.
To serve, reheat the pasta gently and serve with a mixed leaf salad.

Roasted Mediterranean Vegetables

This is a beautifully colourful dish of Mediterranean vegetables roasted in olive oil. It's ideal for parties as it keeps well because the vegetables are marinated in olive oil.

Serves 6

3 assorted coloured peppers

1 red onion

6 garlic cloves, peeled

4 large ripe tomatoes

1 medium aubergines

1 large courgette

200ml olive oil

handful of pitted black olives

freshly ground black pepper

Preheat the oven to 230C/Gas8/450F.
Chop the vegetables roughly into bite sized chunks.
Place all the vegetables, except the tomatoes and olives, onto a large baking tray and spread out evenly.
Pour on the olive oil and sprinkle with freshly ground black pepper.
Roast in the centre of the preheated oven for 30 minutes or until the aubergines are cooked.
When the aubergines are cooked, add the tomatoes and the olives.
Stir well and cook for a further 10 minutes.
Serve warm with ciabatta bread to mop up the olive oil.

Sesame Seeded Spiced Noodles

A Thai inspired dish with a hot and slightly sweet flavour.
Very easy to make.

Serves 6

2 heaped tablespoons sesame seeds

3 tablespoons toasted sesame oil

2 heaped tablespoons peanut butter

2 tablespoons shoyu

2 teaspoons chilli pepper sauce

1 teaspoon apple juice concentrate

200gms vermicelli

Dry roast the sesame seeds in a heavy-bottomed pan until
golden.
Stir them continuously to prevent the seeds burning.
Whisk together the toasted sesame seeds, toasted sesame oil,
peanut butter, shoyu, chilli sauce and apple concentrate.
Cook the vermicelli according to the instructions on the
packet (but be careful not to overcook!).
Drain the vermicelli when it is still a denté and place it
immediately into a serving bowl.
Pour the sauce over the vermicelli and mix well.
Serve straight away.

Spicy Red Wine and Bean Paté

This bean paté is made with pinto beans, a speckled brown bean with a nutty flavour, indigenous to Mexico.

Serves 8

225gms pinto beans, dried weight

or

2 x 425gms tinned pinto beans

2 tablespoons tomato paste

100ml red wine

1 tablespoon chilli pepper sauce

1 teaspoon vegetable bouillon powder

1 teaspoon marmite or yeast extract

freshly ground black pepper

Soak the pinto beans overnight in lots of cold water.
Drain and rinse the beans and then cook in fresh water for 30-40 minutes until soft.
If using tinned pinto beans, drain and rinse them before use.
Preheat the oven to 180C/Gas4/350F.
Blend the drained cooked pinto beans in a food processor with all of the other ingredients to a smooth consistency.
Add freshly ground black pepper to taste.
Pour the bean mixture into a greased shallow oven proof dish.
Cover with foil and bake for one hour.
Chill the paté before serving.

Golden Tofu Nuggets

Thes nuggets are very moreish and are best eaten straight from the oven.

Serves 6

Tofu

570gms plain tofu, (2 packets)

100gms brown rice flour to coat the tofu cubes

Marinade

200ml shoyu

400ml apple juice

50gms piece of fresh ginger root

freshly ground black pepper

Garlic Oil

5 garlic cloves peeled

275ml sunflower oil

Preheat the oven to 180C/Gas4/350F.
Drain off the liquid surrounding the tofu and cut the tofu into 2cm cubes.
Spread the tofu cubes evenly over the bottom of a deep baking dish.

Marinade

To make the marinade, mix the shoyu and apple juice together. To extract the juice from the ginger, grate the ginger into a bowl.

Then take the grated ginger into the palm of your hand and squeeze the juice into the shoyu and apple juice mixture.
Add lots of freshly ground pepper.
Pour the marinade over the tofu cubes.
Cover the baking dish with foil.
Bake the tofu cubes in the preheated oven for 30 minutes.
Remove the baked tofu from the oven and allow to cool.
Drain off the marinade and reserve for the sauce.

Garlic Oil

To make the garlic oil, place the peeled garlic cloves in a blender.
Add the sunflower oil and blend until the garlic is well amalgamated with the oil.
Pour the garlic oil onto a shallow baking tray.

Turn up the oven to 230C/Gas8/450F.
Put the brown rice flour into a bowl.
Roll the baked tofu cubes in the rice flour and place the coated tofu cubes on the garlic oiled baking tray.
Bake in the preheated oven for 15 minutes or until golden.

Sauce

To make the sauce, put the marinade into a small saucepan and boil rigourously until the liquid has reduced by half.
Serve the nuggets hot with the sauce drizzled over them, on a bed of shredded iceberg lettuce.

Pesto Toast

This is one of the most popular light dishes at Demuths. You will need a jar of pesto, bread, tomatoes, avocado and mozzarella to make this delicious combination.

Serves 4

4 slices granary bread

4 tablespoons pesto

4 tomatoes, sliced

1 avocado, peeled and sliced

120gms mozzarella cheese, sliced

Toast the slices of granary bread on one side only.
Spread the untoasted sides with pesto and top with sliced tomato, sliced avocado and finish off with sliced mozzarella.
Place under a hot grill and grill until the mozzarella begins to bubble and turns golden.
Eat at once.

Toasted Olive Bread topped with Sun Dried Tomatoes

Serves 8

> 1 small loaf olive bread
>
> 125gms sun-dried tomatoes, not in oil
>
> 150ml olive oil
>
> 3 garlic cloves, peeled and finely chopped
>
> 1 teaspoon pink peppercorns
>
> 1 teaspoon green peppercorns

Cut the sun-dried tomatoes into small pieces with a pair of kitchen scissors.
Soak the tomatoes in boiling water until they have rehydrated.
Strain off the water and retain it for stock.
Now add to the tomatoes the olive oil, the finely chopped garlic and the peppercorns.
Mix well and leave to marinate.
To serve, slice the olive bread into 8 slices and toast one side only.
Turn over and spread the untoasted sides with the sundried tomato mixture.
Place under a hot grill until the tomatoes begin to brown and serve at once.
Any left over tomato mix will keep in the fridge for a few weeks, providing the tomatoes are well covered in olive oil.

Soups

Stilton and Celery Soup

The richness of the stilton goes wonderfully with the nuttiness of the celery. This soup is best made in the late summer with green celery straight from the garden, which has a much stonger flavour than the white forced celery that you can buy all the year round.

Serves 6

1 bunch celery, washed and chopped including the leaves

25gms butter

1 large onion, peeled and chopped

1 litre vegetable stock

110gms Stilton cheese

150ml single cream

½ teaspoon celery seeds

sea salt and freshly ground blackpepper

Melt the butter in a large saucepan.
Add the chopped onion and sauté until the onion is soft.
Add the chopped celery and sauté for a few minutes, stirring frequently to prevent the vegetables from browning.
Add the stock, bring to the boil and then turn down and simmer for 15 minutes or until the celery is soft.
Crumble the stilton into the soup, then add the cream and the celery seeds and stir until the stilton has melted.
Liquidise to a smooth consistency.
Reheat.
Season with sea salt and freshly ground black pepper to taste.

Broccoli, Pea and Fresh Mint Soup

This soup is a brilliant green colour, best made with fresh peas. If using fresh peas boil up the pea pods with water in a separate saucepan and include in the vegetable stock.

Serves 6

2 tablespoons sunflower oil

1 onion, peeled and chopped

2 garlic cloves, peeled and chopped

1 head broccoli, chopped

400gms peas, podded

1 litre vegetable stock

2 tablespoons lemon juice

1 tablespoon chopped fresh mint

sea salt and freshly ground black pepper

In a large saucepan, fry the chopped onion and garlic in the sunflower oil until soft and translucent.
Add the broccoli, peas and vegetable stock. Bring to the boil and simmer for 20 minutes.
Add the lemon juice and chopped fresh mint.
Liquidise the soup to a smooth consistency.
Reheat.
Season with sea salt and freshly ground black pepper.

Butterbean and Mushroom Soup

This is a clear soup. If using dried butterbeans remember to soak them overnight. If using tinned butterbeans make sure that they are sugar-free.

Serves 6

125gms dried butterbeans

or

1 x 425gm tin butterbeans

1 onion, finely sliced

3 garlic cloves, peeled and crushed

55ml sunflower oil

200gms mushrooms, finely sliced

75ml shoyu

1 litre water

freshly ground black pepper

Soak the dried butter beans overnight.
After soaking, drain and rinse.
Cook them in plenty of water until tender.
If you are using tinned buttterbeans, drain and rinse well before adding them to the soup.
Sauté the sliced onions and garlic in the sunflower oil until soft and translucent.
Add the finely sliced mushrooms to the onions and cook for a few minutes.
Then add the cooked or tinned and drained butterbeans.
Add the shoyu and the water.
If the soup is too thick add a little more water.
Cook gently for 20 minutes and then season to taste.

Carrot and Ginger Soup

A vibrant orange coloured soup, for those who love fresh ginger.

Serves 6

25gms sunflower margarine

1 large onion, sliced

800gms carrots, peeled and chopped

1 medium potato, peeled and chopped

2 stalks of celery, chopped

1 litre water

1 tablespoon lemon juice

1 tablespoon vegetable bouillon powder

½ teaspoon ground ginger

5cm piece of fresh ginger root

sea salt and freshly ground black pepper

fresh chopped coriander, for decoration

Melt the sunflower margarine in a large saucepan.
Add the sliced onion and fry until soft and translucent.
Add the chopped carrots, potato and celery to the cooked onions.
Stir well and cook for a few minutes.
Add the water, lemon juice, ground ginger and bouillon powder and bring to the boil.
Simmer slowly until all the vegetables are soft.
The easiest way to extract the ginger juice is by using the fine side of a hand grater and grating the ginger, including its skin, into a bowl.

Then take all the ginger into your hand and squeeze hard over
the bowl, until all of the juice is extracted.
Mix the ginger juice into the soup.
Liquidise the soup to a smooth consistency.
Add a little more water if necessary.
Reheat
Season with sea salt and freshly ground black pepper.
Decorate with freshly chopped coriander.

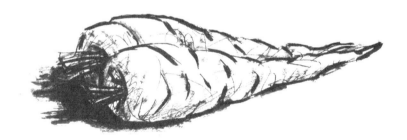

Cucumber, Sorrel and Pea Soup

This is a light summer soup to serve either hot or cold.
Sorrel has the flavour of gooseberries and the acidity of
lemon juice.

Serves 6

1 onion, peeled and chopped

25gms sunflower margarine

1 cucumber, peeled and diced

1 litre vegetable stock

1 handful sorrel

100gms podded peas

sea salt and freshly ground black pepper

Fry the chopped onion gently in the sunflower margarine
making sure the onion does not brown.
Add 2/3 of the peeled and diced cucumber, stir and cook for a
further 5 minutes with the lid on.
Add the vegetable stock and bring to the boil, then add the
sorrel leaves and take the soup off the heat.
Cool and then liquidise until smooth.
Add sea salt and freshly ground black pepper to taste.
In a separate saucepan blanch the peas in boiling water.
Then add the blanched peas and the remaining cucumber
cubes to the soup.
Reheat the soup until hot enough to serve.
To serve cold, chill the soup well and serve with a couple of ice
cubes in each helping.

Lettuce Soup

This soup is best made with a home grown, chlorophyl packed, cos lettuce full of flavour and colour.

Serves 6

1 onion, peeled and chopped

3 garlic cloves, peeled and chopped

25gms butter

1 head Cos lettuce, shredded

250gms potatoes, peeled and chopped

1 litre water

2 teaspoons vegetable bouillon powder

sea salt and freshly ground black pepper

In a large saucepan, fry the chopped onion and garlic in the butter until soft and translucent, but not brown.
Add the chopped potato and the shredded Cos lettuce to the cooked onion and garlic.
Stir well and sauté for a few minutes.
Add the water and the bouillon powder, bring to the boil and simmer until the potatoes are soft.
Allow to cool and then liquidise to a smooth consistency.
Reheat.
Season with sea salt and freshly ground black pepper.

French Onion Soup with Garlic Croutons

The flavour and colour of French onion soup comes from the very slow caramelizing of the onions. It will take at least one hour to make. Serve with garlic croutons.

Serves 6

Soup

2 large onions, very finely chopped (approx 1 kg in weight)

4 tablespoons olive oil

2 garlic cloves, very finely chopped

1 tablespoon chopped fresh parsley

1 heaped teaspoon soft brown sugar

1½ litres boiling water

2 tablespoons shoyu

2 teaspoons marmite or yeast extract

1 tablespoon vegetable bouillon powder

2 tablespoons dry sherry

freshly ground black pepper

Garlic Croutons

3 slices wholewheat bread, cut into cubes

2 tablespoons olive oil

25gms sunflower margarine

2 garlic cloves, crushed

Soup

Fry the chopped onions in the olive oil on a very low heat in a large heavy bottomed saucepan for approximately 45 minutes, stirring frequently.
When the onions are golden brown and beginning to caramelize, add the chopped garlic, sugar and parsley.
Continue to cook for a further 10 minutes, stirring frequently.
Mix the shoyu, marmite and bouillon powder in with the boiling water and add to the onion mixture.
Simmer for a further 10 minutes.
Remove from the heat and add the sherry and lots of freshly ground black pepper.

Garlic croutons

Melt the margarine with the olive oil in a small frying pan.
Add the crushed garlic and fry the bread cubes until golden, turning often.
Remove the croutons from the oil with a slatted spatula and drain them on kitchen paper.
To serve, place the croutons in the bottom of each soup bowl and pour the hot soup over them.

Parsnip and Apple Soup

The sweetness of the parsnips is offset by the tartness of the
cooking apple to make a delicious creamy soup.

Serves 6

1 medium onion, peeled and chopped

25gms butter

3 medium parsnips, peeled and chopped

1 medium cooking apple, peeled, cored and chopped

750ml water

2 teaspoons vegetable bouillon powder

250ml milk

2 tablespoons chopped fresh parsley

sea salt and freshly ground black pepper

Sauté the chopped onion in the butter until soft.
Add the chopped parsnips and cooking apple.
Stir well and sauté for a few minutes.
Add the water, the bouillon powder and the milk and simmer
until the parsnips and apple are cooked.
Liquidise the soup to a smooth consistency.
Season to taste.
Decorate with freshly chopped parsley.
Serve hot with crusty bread.

Sopa di Panela

This Spanish chickpea soup is best made in the summer with lots of freshly picked mint and parsley.

Serves 6

250gms dried chickpeas

or

2 x 425gms tins of sugar free chickpeas

2 garlic cloves, peeled and crushed

4 tablespoons olive oil

1 litre water

1 tablespoon vegetable bouillon powder

1 tablespoon lemon juice

1 handful fresh mint leaves

2 tablespoons chopped fresh parsley

sea salt and freshly ground black pepper

Soak the dried chickpeas overnight.
After soaking drain and rinse well.
Cook them in plenty of water for two hours.
If you are using tinned chickpeas, drain and rinse them well before adding to the soup.
In a large saucepan sauté the crushed garlic in the olive oil.
Add the cooked chickpeas, the water, the vegetable bouillon powder, the lemon juice and the fresh herbs, leaving aside some mint for decoration.
Cook for 10 minutes until all the ingredients are amalgamated.
Leave to cool and then liquidise in a food processor until silky smooth.
Season with sea salt and freshly gound pepper to taste.
Serve hot, decorated with freshly picked mint leaves.

Spicy Peanut, Mushroom and Parsnip Soup

This soup has a creamy texture and a chilli sweet flavour.

Serves 6

1 medium onion, chopped

2 tablespoons sunflower oil

1 teaspoon ground cumin

1 teaspoon ground coriander

1 teaspoon turmeric

200gms mushrooms, sliced

2 medium parsnips, peeled and chopped

1 litre water

1 teaspoon vegetable bouillon powder

2 tablespoons peanut butter

2 tablespoons lemon juice

½ teaspoon chilli powder

sea salt and freshly ground black pepper

Fry the onion in the sunflower oil until soft and beginning to brown.
Add the spices, stir well and fry for a minute.
Add the sliced mushrooms and fry for a few more minutes.
Add the parsnips, vegetable bouillon powder and water, bring to the boil and simmer until the parsnips are soft.
Add the peanut butter, lemon juice and chilli powder and stir.
Liquidise until smooth, adding more liquid if the soup is too thick.
Reheat and season to taste with sea salt and freshly ground black pepper.

Red Lentil and Apricot Soup

A hearty, warming, winter soup.

Serves 6

125gms red split lentils

100gms dried apricot halves

1 large potato, peeled and chopped

1 litre water

1 tablespoon vegetable bouillon powder

2 tablespoons lemon juice

2 teaspoons ground cumin

sea salt and freshly ground black pepper

chopped fresh parsley for decoration

Place all the ingredients except for the salt and pepper in a thick bottomed saucepan.
Cook the potato and lentils until they are soft, stirring regularly to prevent the lentils sticking to the bottom of the saucepan and burning.
Liquidise the soup to a smooth consistency adding a little more water if necessary.
Reheat.
Season with sea salt and freshly ground pepper and decorate with fresh parsley.

Main Dishes

Spring Onion and Potato Puff Pastry Slice

A simple supper dish, served hot with a crisp green salad.
The recipe uses frozen puff pastry, so remember to defrost it in
good time.

Serves 6

4 medium potatoes, peeled and sliced

300ml milk

1 bunch spring onions

25gms melted butter

1 tablespoon finely chopped parsley

salt and freshly ground black pepper

150ml single cream

300gms puff pastry, unfrozen

Preheat the oven to 200C/Gas6/400F.
In a thick bottomed saucepan cook the peeled, sliced potatoes
in enough milk to cover them and add a pinch of salt.
Chop the spring onions and fry them lightly in 2/3 of the butter.
Drain the potatoes and add the cooked spring onions along
with the chopped parsley, salt, freshly ground black pepper
and the cream.
Grease a large deep baking dish.
Roll out ½ of the puff pastry and line the bottom of the dish
with it keeping the sides of the dish clear.
Spread the potato cream mixture onto the pastry.
Roll out the remaining pastry and cover the potato mixture with it.
Using a pastry brush paint the top with the remaining butter.
Cook in the middle of the preheated oven for 40minutes or
until golden in colour.

Creamy Cashewnut and Coconut Curry

This curry is rich and creamy. The creaminess coming from the coconut and the richness from the rather extravagant quantity of cashews.

Serves 6

3 tablespoons sunflower oil

2 medium onions, thinly sliced

2 teaspoons ground coriander

1 teaspoon ground cumin

½ teaspoon turmeric

¼ teaspoon chilli powder

2 garlic cloves, finely chopped

1 large yellow pepper, thinly sliced

1 medium green pepper, thinly sliced

6 celery sticks, chopped

250gms unsalted cashewnuts

8 tomatoes, skinned and chopped

½ packet creamed coconut, dissolved in 500mls boiling water

2 tablespoons lime juice

sea salt and freshly ground black pepper

2 tablespoons freshly chopped coriander

Skin the tomatoes by putting them in a bowl of boiling water and leaving them for a few minutes until the skins are easy to peel off.

In a wok or a large heavy bottomed saucepan, fry the sliced onions in the sunflower oil until they begin to brown and caramelise.

Add the spices and the chopped garlic and fry for a few minutes.

Now add the sliced peppers, chopped celery and cashewnuts and stir fry for a few more minutes.

Dissolve the creamed coconut in the boiling water and add to the curry along with the lime juice and the chopped and skinned tomatoes.

Season to taste.

Cover and simmer for 30 minutes.

Just before serving add the freshly chopped coriander.

Jerusalem Artichoke, Courgette and Tomato Pasta Bake

Jerusalem artichokes were brought back from the New World in the seventeenth century. The name is taken from the Italian "girasole articocco"- sunflower artichoke, which was altered to Jerusalem. The plant has leaves like a sunflower and edible tubers like very knobbly potatoes. They have the flavour of globe artichokes and a lovely crisp texture. The only drawback to Jerusalem artichokes is that they can cause flatulence. Yikes!

Serves 6

500gms jerusalem artichokes

2 medium onions, chopped

4 garlic cloves, finely chopped

4 tablespoons olive oil

1 small aubergine, cubed

1 medium red pepper, sliced

1 medium yellow pepper, sliced

2 medium courgettes, chopped

8 tomatoes, skinned and chopped

1 tablespoon shoyu

1 tablespoon tomato puree

1 teaspoon chilli pepper sauce

1 tablespoon freshly chopped oregano

sea salt and freshly ground black pepper

250gms penne pasta

200gms cheddar cheese, grated

Preheat the oven to 220C/Gas7/425F.

Boil the artichokes in their skins for about 10 minutes until the skins are easy to peel off.

Drain, cool, peel and chop the artichokes into chunks.

In a wok or large saucepan, fry the chopped onions in the olive oil until they are soft and translucent.

Add the cubed aubergine and the chopped garlic and fry on a high heat until the aubergine is golden.

You may need to add more oil as aubergine is notoriously thirsty.

Add the sliced peppers, chopped courgettes and stir fry for a few minutes.

Add the peeled chopped artichokes, the skinned and chopped tomatoes, shoyu, tomato puree, chilli pepper sauce and the freshly chopped oregano.

Season to taste with sea salt and add lots of freshly ground black pepper.

Cover and simmer until the mixture reaches the consistency of a thick pasta sauce.

Add water if the mixture is too dry.

Cook the penne pasta in plenty of boiling water a denté.

Drain the pasta and mix it with the pasta sauce.

Spoon into a large gratin dish and sprinkle with grated cheese.

Bake in the preheated oven for 20 minutes or until golden.

Carrot Roulade with Cream Cheese and Pink Peppercorns

This is a lovely, light summer roulade. The pink peppercorns give the cream cheese filling an unusual bitter sweet taste and a crunchy texture.

Serves 4

Roulade

4 free range eggs, separated

250gms carrots, peeled and chopped

1 teaspoon vegetable bouillon powder

pinch of sea salt

Filling

175gms cream cheese

1 tablespoon pink peppercorns

Preheat the oven to 200C/Gas6/400F.
Grease and line a swiss roll tin (approx 30cm x 20cm) with greased baking parchment.
Peel the carrots, roughly chop and boil until tender.
Drain the cooked carrots and leave to cool, then purée in a food processor until smooth.
Add the egg yolks, bouillon powder and salt.
Blend on a low speed until the eggs are well amalgamated.
Whisk the egg whites until just stiff, but not dry.
Fold the stiffly beaten egg whites gently into the carrot mixture, until no white is left showing.

Spread the roulade mixture evenly over the prepared swiss roll tin.

Bake the roulade in the centre of the preheated oven for 10 to 15 minutes or until it is spongy to the touch.

Leave the roulade to cool for at least 1 hour before filling.

To turn out the roulade, cut a piece of greaseproof paper a little larger than the swiss roll tin and lay it on a baking sheet. Turn the roulade onto the greaseproof paper and peel off the backing baking parchment.

When the roulade is completely cold, spread the cream cheese evenly over the surface of the roulade using a hot palette knife, then sprinkle over the whole pink peppercorns.

Using the greaseproof paper and holding it by the long edge, roll the roulade up lengthways.

This roulade can be served warm or cold.

Refrigerate before serving or gently warm in a low oven.

Mozzarella, Aubergine and Tomato Gratin

This gratin is very delicious, but takes a while to make as the aubergine slices need to be fried first in olive oil. Vegetarian parmesan cheese is now available in wholefood shops.

Serves 6

4 medium aubergines

unbleached white flour, for coating the aubergines

150ml olive oil

500gms mozzarella cheese

50gms vegetarian parmesan, or strong cheddar, grated

Tomato Sauce

1 onion, finely chopped

2 garlic cloves, peeled and finely chopped

2 tablespoons olive oil

900gms tomatoes, chopped

1 tablespoon tomato puree

1 handful fresh basil, chopped

sea salt and freshly ground black pepper

Preheat the oven to 200C/Gas6/400F.
Remove the stalky ends of the aubergines and thinly slice them lengthways.
Dip each slice in the flour, coating both sides.
Heat the olive oil in large frying pan and fry the aubergine slices until golden on both sides.
Drain the fried aubergine on kitchen paper.

Tomato Sauce

Fry the chopped onion and garlic in the olive oil until golden.
Then add the chopped tomatoes and the tomato puree.
Simmer for 30 minutes.
Liquidise to a smooth conistency.
Add the chopped basil.
Season to taste with sea salt and freshly ground black pepper.

Place the aubergine slices in the bottom of a greased, shallow, oven-proof dish, so that they cover the bottom but do not overlap.
Slice the mozzarella cheese and place a slice of mozzarella on top of each aubergine slice.
Cover with tomato sauce and sprinkle with grated parmesan or a strong cheddar cheese.
Bake in the centre of the preheated oven for 30 minutes or until golden brown.

Fennel and Leeks à la Niçoise

Leeks are added to this niçoise to tone down the aniseed flavour
of the fennel, which some people can find overpoweringly strong.

Serves 4

2 large fennel bulbs, quartered

2 leeks, sliced in 2cm chunks

Sauce

1 medium onion, chopped

2 garlic cloves, finely chopped

2 tablespoons olive oil

1 small carrot, peeled and finely chopped

1 stalk of celery, finely chopped

6 tomatoes, skinned and chopped

200ml dry white wine

bouquet garni

sea salt and freshly ground black pepper

½ tablespoon demerara sugar

110gms pitted black olives, halved

50gms mature cheddar, grated

Preheat the oven to 180C/Gas4/350F.
In separate saucepans, blanch the quartered fennel and the
leek chunks, until just tender.

The fennel takes about 10 minutes and the leeks about 5.
Leave them to drain while you make the sauce.

Sauce

Sauté the chopped onion and the garlic in the olive oil until the
onion is soft.
Add the finely chopped carrot and fry for a few more minutes.
Add the skinned chopped tomatoes, the bouquet garni and the
white wine.
Simmer for 40 minutes on a very low heat.
Season with sea salt and freshly ground black pepper and
sweeten with sugar to taste.

Place the blanched fennel and leeks in a gratin dish.
Sprinkle over the halved olives and cover with the sauce.
Sprinkle with grated cheddar and bake in the preheated oven
for 30 minutes.

Focaccia with Verdura Piccante Sauce

A simple to make Italian bread which can be flavoured with herbs of your choice. Sage gives the focaccia a robust flavour.

Serves 6

Foccacia

7gms dried yeast

250ml warm water

375gms strong unbleached white flour, sieved

1 teaspoon sea salt

2 teaspoons dried sage

3 tablespoons olive oil

salt crystals to sprinkle on top

Verdura Piccante Sauce

1 head broccoli

10 ripe tomatoes, skinned and finely chopped

2 medium red onions, finely sliced

2 tablespoons olive oil

3 garlic cloves, peeled and finely chopped

2 tablespoons red wine

2 red chillies, de-seeded and finely chopped

75gms black olives, pitted and chopped

500gms passata, (blended, sieved tomatoes)

1 teaspoon marmite or yeast extract

3 tablespoons fresh basil, chopped

sea salt and freshly ground black pepper

Focaccia

Mix the yeast with the warm water in a bowl and stir well.
Cover with cling-film and leave in a warm place until it forms a frothy head, which will take about 10 minutes.
Mix the salt and herbs into the sieved flour.
Add 1 tablespoon of olive oil to the yeast mixture and pour into the flour mixture.
Mix well with your hands into a soft ball.
Turn out onto a floured surface.
Knead well until the dough is springy and elastic.
Return the dough to a large oiled bowl.
Cover the bowl with cling-film and leave in a warm place, for approximately 45 minutes until the dough has doubled in size.
Preheat the oven to 190C/Gas5/375F.
Grease a baking sheet.
Roll out the dough into a flat, thick, pizza shape, approx 30cm wide and 1cm thick.
Place the focaccia onto the greased baking sheet and make dimples on the top with your fingers.
Brush the top with the remaining olive oil and sprinkle with salt crystals.
Leave to rest for 10 minutes.
Bake in the preheated oven for 35minutes or until golden and the bottom of the focaccia sounds hollow when tapped.
While the focaccia is baking, make the sauce.

Verdura Piccante Sauce

Split the head of broccoli into florets and steam them until they are just tender.

Immerse the tomatoes in a bowl of boiling water for a few minutes, then remove, skin and finely chop.

In a large saucepan sauté the sliced onions in the olive oil until soft.

Add the chopped garlic and the wine and cook for a few more minutes.

Add the skinned and chopped tomatoes, the chopped chillies, the chopped olives, the passata and the marmite.

Cook for about 10 minutes.

Add the steamed broccoli and the chopped fresh basil and season well.

Split the warm freshly baked focaccia and fill it with the Verdura Piccante sauce.

Parsnip and Cashew Roasts with Red Onion and Basil Sauce

The sweetness of the parsnips and the crunchiness of the cashews combine to make a festive roast. You will need six college pudding moulds or ramekins to cook the individual roasts.

Serves 6

Roasts

4 medium sized parsnips, peeled and chopped

1 medium onion, finely chopped

3 tablespoons sunflower oil

225gms cashew nuts, crumbed

110gms wholemeal breadcrumbs

2 teaspoons dried basil

150ml vegetable stock

2 teaspoons shoyu

sea salt and freshly ground black pepper

Filling

150gms mushrooms, sliced

2 garlic cloves, finely chopped

3 tablespoons sunflower oil

Sauce

2 medium red onions, finely chopped

3 tablespoons sunflower oil

570ml vegetable stock

1 heaped teaspoon cornflour

1 teaspoon shoyu

1 tablespoon chopped fresh basil or 1 teaspoon dried basil

sea salt and freshly ground black pepper

Roasts
Preheat the oven to 180C/Gas4/350F.
Grease the pudding moulds and cut a disc of greaseproof paper to fit in the bottom of each pudding mould.
Peel, chop, and cook the parsnips in water until soft in the centre.
Drain and mash well.
Fry the chopped onion in the sunflower oil until soft.
Put the cooked onion in a large mixing bowl and add the mashed parsnip and mix well, then add the crumbed cashew nuts, breadcrumbs, dried basil, vegetable stock and shoyu.
Mix well and leave the mixture to stand until the liquid is absorbed.
The consistency of the mix should be stiff, but moist. If the mixture is too dry add a little more water.
Add sea salt and freshly ground black pepper to taste.

Filling
Heat the remaining sunflower oil and fry the mushrooms and garlic until the mushrooms are soft.
Fill the pudding moulds halfway with the nut mixture and then a layer of mushroom mixture, divided equally between the pudding moulds.
Then fill up to the brim with the remaining nut mixture and press down firmly.
Place the filled pudding moulds on a baking tray, cover with silver foil and bake in the centre of the oven for 45 minutes.
Leave the roasts to cool in the moulds.
When cool run a palette knife around the edge of each roast and turn out onto an oven proof dish.

Sauce

Fry the red onions in the sunflower oil until soft and translucent.

Mix the cornflour with a little of the cold stock to make a smooth paste.

Add the rest of the stock to the cooked onions and bring to the boil.

Turn down and simmer until the stock has been reduced by 1/3rd.

Now add the shoyu and the basil.

Lastly, whisk in the cornflour paste.

Bring to the boil and simmer for a few minutes, until the cornflour has thickened the sauce.

Add sea salt and freshly ground black pepper to taste.

Warm the roasts gently and serve surrounded with the red onion and basil sauce.

Fritatta Primavera with Fresh Oregano

This is a traditional Italian baked omelette, very light and colourful.

Serves 4

½ small green pepper, thinly sliced into strips

½ small yellow pepper, thinly sliced into strips

50gms mangetout peas, topped and tailed

3 spring onions, thinly sliced lengthways

1 small courgette, cut into fine sticks

50gms peas

2 tablespoons olive oil

4 free range eggs

150ml milk

1 tablespoon fresh oregano, chopped

125gms mozzarella cheese, cut into strips

sea salt and freshly ground black pepper

fresh oregano, chopped to garnish

Preheat oven to 200C/Gas6/400F.
Grease and line a 23cm flan tin with baking parchment and grease this too.
Heat the olive oil in a wok or large saucepan and lightly stir fry all the prepared vegetables.
Meanwhile, whisk together the eggs and milk with the sea salt, freshly ground pepper and chopped fresh oregano.

Arrange the stir fried vegetables evenly into the greased, lined flan tin.
Arrange the strips of mozzarella on top like the spokes of a wheel.
Carefully pour on the egg mixture.

Bake for approximately 20 minutes in the centre of the preheated oven until firm and golden .
Serve warm, garnished with fresh oregano.

Matar Paneer

This pea and curd cheese curry is made with vegetarian paneer, an Indian curd cheese, which is tasteless before it is cooked but it soaks up the flavours from the curry and has a lovely chewy texture. You can buy paneer from Indian grocery stores.

Serves 6

6 tomatoes, skinned and chopped finely

2 medium onions, thinly sliced

50gms butter

450gms peas

250gms vegetarian paneer, cut into cubes

1 tablespoon curry powder

1 tablespoon black mustard seed

1 tablespoon ground cumin

2 teaspoons ground coriander

500ml water

2 bay leaves

1 teaspoon sea salt

1 tablespoon lemon juice

1 teaspoon garam masala

freshly ground black pepper

Pour boiling water over the tomatoes.
Leave for a few minutes and then skin and chop them.
In a thick bottomed, large saucepan, cook the thinly sliced onions in the butter until they begin to brown and caramelise.

Then add all the spices, except the garam masala.
Cook for a few minutes stirring continuously until the mustard seeds start to pop.
(Be very careful not to let the spices burn.)
Add the peas and the chopped tomatoes and cook for a further few minutes until well coated in the spices, then add the paneer and stir gently in.
Now add the water, the bay leaves and the salt.
Bring to the boil, turn the heat down and simmer gently for 25 minutes.
At the last minute add the lemon juice and the garam masala and stir in well.
Season to taste.
Serve with basmati rice and a sweet mango chutney.

Mushroom and Aubergine Bourguignonne with Seitan

A wonderful winter warmer, made with seitan which is braised wheat gluten. Sometimes known as 'mock duck'.

Serves 6

450gms button mushrooms

450gms aubergines, cubed

1 small red pepper, sliced

1 small yellow pepper, sliced

2 onions, finely sliced

8 tablespoons olive oil

Bourguignonne Sauce

1 heaped tablespoon unbleached white flour

600ml red wine

350gms seitan, drained and diced

3 garlic cloves, peeled and chopped

1 teaspoon thyme

2 bay leaves

1 teaspoon marmite or yeast extract

sea salt and freshly ground black pepper

Preheat the oven to 150C/Gas2/300F.
Heat half the olive oil in a large frying pan or a wok and fry the mushrooms, the cubed aubergines and the sliced peppers until golden.
Put the remaining olive oil into an oven-proof casserole dish,

add the sliced onion and fry until soft but not browned.

Bourguignonne Sauce
Sprinkle the flour onto the cooked onions and stir to a smooth paste.
Add the red wine a little at a time, stirring all the time until you have a smooth, thin sauce.
Add the cooked mushroom and aubergine mixture and the diced seitan to the sauce and stir well.
Lastly add the chopped garlic, herbs and marmite and bring to the boil.
Place a tight fitting lid on the casserole dish and cook in the preheated oven for 2 hours.

Smoked Tofu and Mushroom Pie

A rich savoury vegan pie with a puff pastry top and a smoked tofu and mushroom filling.

Serves 6

1 large onion, finely chopped

2 tablespoons sunflower oil

500gms mushrooms, sliced

3 garlic cloves, finely chopped

220gms smoked tofu, cubed

200gms puff pastry

Sauce

1 tablespoon shoyu

1 level tablespoon marmite or yeast extract

1 heaped teaspoon vegetable bouillon powder

freshly ground black pepper

3 heaped teaspoons cornflour

500ml boiling water

Preheat the oven to 220C/Gas7/425F.
Grease a 25cm/1 litre oval rimmed pie dish.
Heat the sunflower oil in a thick bottomed large saucepan, add the chopped onions and sauté until soft.
Add the sliced mushrooms and fry until they begin to brown.
Add the garlic and the cubed smoked tofu and stir fry for a couple of minutes.

Sauce

Mix the shoyu, marmite and bouillon powder with a little boiling water and add to the tofu and mushroom mixture.
Pour the remaining boiling water into the tofu mixture, bring to the boil and allow to simmer gently.
Mix the cornflour with a little cold water to make a smooth · paste.
Then add the cornflour paste, little by little to the simmering tofu mixture, stirring all the time until the sauce thickens.
Add plenty of freshly ground black pepper.

Allow the tofu mushroom mixture to cool slightly and then fill the pie dish.
The mixture should come up to the lip of the pie dish.
Roll out the puff pastry, about 2.5cms larger than the pie-dish, then cut out a 2.5cms strip to fit the edge of the dish.
Dampen the edge of the dish with a little water and stick down the pastry strip firmly.
Now dampen the strip and press the rest of the pastry over the pie to form a lid.
Trim off any excess pastry.
Flute the edges and make a steam hole in the middle of the pie.
Decorate with shapes made from any left over pastry.
Brush the top with a little sunflower oil.
Bake in the preheated oven for approximately 20 minutes until crisp and golden.

Red Onion and Red Leicester Cheese Tart

This tart is very rich, the red onions are sweeter than ordinary onions. The combination of the red cheese and the red onions gives the tart a lovely purple colour.

Serves 6

Pastry

220gms plain flour

50gms butter or margarine

50gms vegetable shortening

pinch of sea salt

4 tablespoons cold water

Filling

25gms butter

450gms red onions, peeled and thinly sliced

3 free range eggs

100gms red leicester cheese, grated

140ml single cream

sea salt and freshly ground black pepper

Pastry

Place the flour and salt in a food processor and mix well.
Dice the fat and add to the flour and mix until it resembles breadcrumbs.
Add the cold water a little at a time and mix for only a few seconds until the pastry forms a soft ball.
Remove the pastry from the food processor.
Wrap and leave in the fridge for at least 1 hour.

Filling

Preheat the oven to 200C/Gas6/400F.

Melt the butter in a heavy bottomed saucepan.

Add the thinly sliced red onions, stir well, cover and sauté for about 10 minutes until the onions are soft.

Remove the lid and fry the onions on a higher heat, until they are lightly browned.

In a mixing bowl, whisk the eggs, mix in the grated cheese, cream and season with a pinch of sea salt and lots of freshly ground pepper.

Roll out the pastry on a lightly floured surface to fit a 23cm flan case.

Mix the cooked onions with the egg and cheese mixture and pour into the pastry case.

Bake in centre of the preheated oven for approximately 40 minutes or until the top is firm and golden.

Oriental Stir Fry with Marinated Tofu

The joy of a stir fry is that you can use whatever vegetables you like.

Serves 4

Tofu

285gms plain tofu, (one pack) cut into bite sized cubes

Marinade

1 tablespoon toasted sesame oil

2 tablespoons shoyu

2 tablespoons dry sherry

1 tablespoon sweet chilli sauce

Stir Fry

1 tablespoon toasted sesame oil

4 garlic cloves, peeled and finely chopped

1 piece ginger, peeled and finely chopped

1 medium carrot, peeled and finely sliced

50gms shitake mushrooms, finely sliced

125gms mangetout peas, topped and tailed

125gms mini sweetcorn spears, cut in half diagonally

1 red pepper, cut in strips

100gms beansprouts

lots of freshly ground black pepper

Marinade

In a bowl, mix the toasted sesame oil, shoyu, sherry and chilli sauce together.

Add the cubed tofu and mix the cubes into the marinade.

Leave for 1 hour stirring often to ensure that all the tofu is evenly marinated.

While the tofu is marinating prepare the vegetables for the stir fry.

Stir Fry

Heat the toasted sesame oil in a wok.

Add the garlic, ginger and carrot and stir fry on a high heat for a few minutes.

Add the rest of the vegetables except the bean sprouts and stir fry for a few more minutes.

Add the tofu with all the marinade liquid and turn down the heat a little.

Stir fry for a few more minutes until the vegetables are tender, but still crisp.

Lastly add the bean sprouts and lots of freshly ground pepper.

Turn up the heat and stir fry for 1 more minute to heat through the bean sprouts.

Serve at once on a bed of scented Thai rice.

Sundried Tomato and Feta Filo Pie

This is a very rich and delicious summer dish. Serve with a green salad and new potatoes.

Serves 6

175gms sun-dried tomatoes, not in oil

4 tablespoons olive oil

1 large onion, finely sliced

4 red peppers, finely sliced into strips

225gms mushrooms, finely sliced

4 garlic cloves, finely chopped

175gms feta cheese, sliced into strips

freshly ground black pepper

10 sheets of filo pastry, measuring approximately 25cms x 20cms

Preheat the oven to 200C/Gas6/400F.
Grease an oven proof dish approximately 25cm x 20cm in size.
Soak the sun-dried tomatoes in boiling water until they are reconstituted, (about 10 minutes).
Drain, retaining the tomato juice for stock and chop the tomatoes up roughly with a pair of kitchen scissors.
Heat 2 tablespoons of the olive oil in a wok or large saucepan and sauté the sliced onions and red peppers until soft.
Remove and put in a bowl for later use.
Heat the remaining oil in the same pan and fry the mushrooms and the garlic until the mushrooms begin to brown.
Add lots of freshly ground pepper.

Place 2 sheets of filo into the greased oven-proof dish and spread the onion and pepper mixture over the filo.
Place a further 2 sheets of filo on top and spread with the mushroom and garlic mixture.
Then another 2 sheets of filo spread with the chopped sun dried tomatoes.
Then another 2 sheets of filo with the feta cheese placed evenly on top.
Lastly cover the top with the last 2 sheets of filo.
With a pastry brush, liberally paint the top of the filo pie with olive oil.
Bake in the preheated oven for 25 minutes or until golden.
Serve warm.

Shallot, Mushroom and Ginger Pancakes

This unusual strongly flavoured filling of shallots, chestnut mushrooms and fresh ginger works very well wrapped in a simple pancake.

Serves 6

Pancakes - makes 12

3 free range eggs

200ml milk

75ml water

2 tablespoons sunflower oil

pinch of salt

110gms plain white flour, sieved

sunflower oil, for frying

Shallot, Mushroom and Ginger Filling

3 tablespoons olive oil

6 shallots, peeled and quartered

3 garlic cloves, finely chopped

400gms chestnut mushrooms, finely sliced

200ml sour cream

2 tablespoons single cream

2 teaspoons shoyu

1 piece fresh ginger root, grated with the peel on

2 tablespoons fresh coriander, chopped

lots of freshly ground black pepper

MAIN DISHES

Pancakes

Place the eggs, milk, water, sunflower oil and salt in a food processor and blend until smooth.

Add the sieved flour and blend again until the mixture is silky in texture.

Cover the mixture and leave to stand in the fridge for 30 minutes.

Filling

In a heavy bottomed saucepan, sauté the quartered shallots in the olive oil until golden.

Add the chopped garlic and the sliced mushrooms and sauté until the mushrooms are cooked.

Remove from the heat.

Add the sour cream, single cream and shoyu, mix well and heat gently.

To extract the juice from the ginger, squeeze the grated ginger in the palm of your hand over the mushroom mixture and mix in well.

Add the chopped fresh coriander and lots of freshly ground black pepper.

To cook the pancakes you will need a non stick rounded frying pan and a non stick spatula.

Heat two teaspoons of sunflower oil in the frying pan, swirl the oil around to cover the whole frying pan and pour the excess oil back into a heat proof jug.

Now pour 2 tablespoons of pancake batter into the centre of the pan over a medium heat and tip the pan from side to side so that the base of the frying pan is evenly coated with batter.

Cook until the underside of the pancake is golden, approximately ½ minute.

Loosen the edges of the pancake with the spatula, shake the pan and flick the pancake over and cook for a further ¼ minute.

Fill the pancakes with the warm shallot, mushroom and ginger mixture and serve at once.

Aubergine and Chickpea Tagine

This recipe comes from Iran where they use copious quantities of cinnamon and nutmeg. Be brave and add the full amount of spices as the aubergine absorbs them and you end up with a richly aromatic dish.

Serves 6

2 onions, chopped

150ml olive oil

3 aubergines, cubed

800gms tinned tomatoes, chopped

425gms tin sugar free chickpeas

½ tablespoon ground nutmeg

1 tablespoon ground cinnamon

sea salt and freshly ground black pepper

Fry the chopped onions in a third of the olive oil until soft and golden in colour.
Remove the onions from the frying pan.
Fry the aubergines in the remaining olive oil, until crisp.
In a large heavy bottomed pan add the cooked onions, the aubergines, the spices and cook for 10 minutes, stirring often to stop the spices catching on the bottom of the pan.
Now add the chopped tinned tomatoes and the tinned, drained chickpeas.
Cook for a further 30 minutes.
Add sea salt and freshly ground black pepper to taste.
Serve with couscous.

Polenta with Char-grilled Peppers and Olives

Polenta is the essential staple ingredient of northern Italy. It is made from yellow maize flour. Try and buy 'quick cook' polenta flour which is much easier to make into polenta, as it needs less stirring.

Serves 6

Polenta

250gms polenta flour

1 teaspoon salt

1 litre water

1 tablespoon olive oil

Char-grilled Peppers

4 medium red peppers

2 medium yellow peppers

2 medium red onions, peeled and finely sliced

2 tablespoons olive oil

8 garlic cloves, very finely chopped

275ml red wine

150ml red grape juice

150gms pitted black olives, halved

lots of freshly ground black pepper

Polenta

First of all you will need to make the polenta, as it takes time to set.

Put 1 litre of water plus the salt and the olive oil into a heavy bottomed, high sided saucepan.

Bring to the boil and then remove from the heat.

Now gradually add the polenta flour, stirring all the time with a whisk or a wooden spoon.

Return the saucepan to the heat, bring to the boil and simmer for 5 minutes, stirring constantly.

The polenta is cooked when it falls away from the sides of the saucepan and is no longer granular in texture.

Pour the cooked polenta mixture onto a large, oiled baking tray.

Spread out to a thickness of 2cms.

Leave until completely cold and solid.

While the polenta is setting, make the char-grilled peppers.

Char-grilled Peppers

Cut the peppers in half and remove the stalks and seeds.

Place them under a hot grill and grill on both sides until blistered and charred all over.

To make peeling the peppers easy, place them in a plastic bag, seal and leave the peppers to sweat in the bag for approximately $1/2$ hour.

The condensation within the bag will make the skins come off easily.

After $1/2$ hour, take the peppers out of the plastic bag, peel off the skins and slice the peeled peppers into strips.

While the peppers are sweating, cook the finely sliced onions
in the olive oil until soft.
Add the garlic and wine and simmer gently for a few minutes
then add the sliced peppers, the halved olives and the red
grape juice.
Simmer for a further few minutes.
Season with lots of freshly ground black pepper.
Cut the polenta into triangular wedges approximately 6 cms
long.
Brush the wedges with olive oil and place under a hot grill until
golden.
To serve, spoon the hot sauce over the grilled polenta triangles
and serve with a mixed leaf salad.

Mushroom, Tarragon and Almond Roast

This roast is perfect for a festive vegan dish and is served with a roasted pepper and tomato sauce.

Serves 6

Roast

1 medium onion, finely chopped

4 tablespoons sunflower oil

350gms mushrooms

200gms ground almonds

300gms fresh breadcrumbs

2 tablespoons fresh chopped tarragon

2 tablespoons shoyu

2 teaspoons vegetable bouillon powder

sea salt and freshly ground black pepper

Sauce

4 large red peppers

500gms passata (blended sieved tomatoes)

2 teaspoons shoyu

freshly ground black pepper

Preheat oven to 200C/Gas6/400F.
Grease and line a 900gm loaf tin with baking parchment.
Sauté the chopped onion in the sunflower oil until golden.
In a food processor finely chop the mushrooms, add them
to the onions and sautée them for a couple of minutes.
Transfer the cooked onions and mushrooms to a big
mixing bowl.
Add the ground almonds, breadcrumbs, chopped fresh
tarragon and the shoyu mixed with the vegetable bouillon
powder.
Mix well.
The consistency of the mix should form a moist ball.
If it is too dry add a little warm water.
Add salt and freshly ground black pepper to taste.
Press the mixture into the prepared loaf tin and bake in
the preheated oven for approximately 45 minutes or until
firm.
Allow to cool slightly before turning out.

Sauce
Cut the peppers in half and discard the seeds.
Place them under a hot grill, and grill on both sides until
the skins begin to blister.
The easiest way to peel the peppers is to place them in a
plastic bag when they are still hot and leave them to sweat
for $\frac{1}{2}$ hour.
Remove them from the bag and peel them easily.
Place the peeled peppers into the food processor.
Add the passata, shoyu and freshly ground black pepper.
Liquidise until smooth.
Reheat and serve with the roast.

Risotto Primavera

A colourful spring risotto made with arborio rice scented with saffron.

Serves 6

2 tablespoons olive oil

1 onion, finely sliced

2 garlic cloves, finely chopped

200gms arborio rice

110gms mangetout peas, topped and tailed

110gms sweetcorn

1 large carrot, peeled and cut into fine strips

1 large courgette, cut into fine sticks

1 large green pepper, finely sliced into strips

½ teaspoon saffron

750ml vegetable stock, boiling

75ml sherry

50gms butter

1 tablespoon fresh chives, chopped

sea salt and freshly ground black pepper

1 tablespoon vegetarian parmesan

Heat the olive oil in a large heavy bottomed saucepan.
Add the sliced onion and garlic and sauté until just soft.
Add the rice and stir well until the grains are coated in oil.
Gradually add the hot stock with the saffron, a ladle at a time.

Stir frequently on a medium heat, allowing the risotto to absorb each ladle of stock, before adding more.
With the last ladle of stock add the prepared vegetables.
Simmer until all the liquid is absorbed and the vegetables are a denté.
Add the sherry, butter and parmesan.
Simmer again for a few minutes, stirring all the time until the sherry has been absorbed but the rice is still moist.
Take the risotto off the heat.
Season to taste and add fresh chopped chives.
Serve at once with parmesan sprinkled over.

Red Wine Goulash

This dish improves if made the day before for the paprika and the wine to marinate into the beans and lentils.
The vegetables should be chunky and although the quantities of wine and sherry are very generous, it is well worth it!

Serves 6

125gms black-eyed bean (dried weight)

1 large onion, sliced

75ml olive oil

3 large carrots, peeled and diced

1 red pepper, sliced

1 green pepper, sliced

2 teaspoons paprika

1½ teaspoons dried basil

1½ teaspoons dried oregano

3 tablespoons tomato paste

1 teaspoon vegetable bouillon powder

500ml boiling water

85gms red split lentils

275ml red wine

75ml sherry

3 tomatoes, skinned and chopped

sea salt and freshly ground black pepper

Soak the black-eyed beans overnight in plenty of cold water.
The next day, drain and cook in plenty of fresh water until just tender.
In a large heavy bottomed saucepan sauté the sliced onion in the olive oil until soft.
Add the diced carrots and the sliced peppers and cook for a few minutes.
Add the paprika and herbs.
Mix the tomato paste and the vegetable bouillon powder with the boiling water and add to the vegetable mixture.
Then add the drained, cooked black-eyed beans and the dried lentils.
Cook on a low heat until the lentils are cooked and the carrots soft.
Stir often and add more water if necessary.
Take care not to let the mixture burn as the lentils absorb a lot of liquid.
Add the wine, sherry and the skinned, chopped tomatoes.
Simmer for a further 10 minutes and season to taste.
Serve with couscous and for non vegans add a dollop of sour cream.

Shittake Mushroom Strudel with Shallot and Mushroom Sauce

Fresh shiitake mushrooms with their robust flavour are now readily available. If you have to use dried, soak well in advance. Chestnut mushrooms so named because of their colour are often organically grown and have a lovely nutty flavour and firm texture. This recipe is ideal for a winter dinner party or for Christmas dinner and will make two strudels.

Serves 8

Strudel

12 shiitake mushrooms, cut into quarters

6 tablespoons olive oil

450gms mushrooms, cut into quarters

450gms leeks, finely shredded including as much green as possible.

75gms walnuts, chopped

225gms cooked white rice

1½ tablespoons shoyu

1 tablespoon chopped fresh oregano

sea salt and freshly ground black pepper

10 sheets unfrozen filo pastry

poppy seeds, to decorate

Sauce

2 tablespoons olive oil

6 shallots, peeled and finely sliced.

225gms chestnut mushrooms, thinly sliced

750ml vegetable stock

2 heaped teaspoons cornflour

1 tablespoon shoyu

1 tablespoon sherry

sea salt and freshly ground black pepper

Strudels
Preheat the oven to 200C/Gas6/400F.
Heat 4 tablespoons of olive oil in a wok or large thick bottomed saucepan.
Add the mushrooms and stir fry for a few minutes.
Add the leeks and fry again, keeping the leeks green.
Add the walnuts, cooked rice, shoyu, oregano and seasoning and mix well.
Remove from the heat and leave to cool.
Divide the mushroom mixture into two, half for each strudel.
Place a sheet of greaseproof paper onto your work surface.
Place a sheet of filo onto the greaseproof paper and brush with a little olive oil.
Repeat with another four sheets of filo.
Spread the layered filo with one half of the mushroom mixture making sure you spread it evenly all over.
Taking hold of the greaseproof paper on the long side of the strudel, roll it up away from you.
Transfer the roll onto a greased baking sheet seam side down.
Brush with olive oil and sprinkle with poppy seeds.
Repeat the process with the second strudel.
Bake in the preheated oven for 20 minutes or until golden.

Sauce
Fry the shallots in the olive oil until brown.
Add the sliced chestnut mushrooms and fry for a few minutes.
Mix the cornflour with a little of the stock to make a paste and add to the sauce along with the stock, shoyu and sherry.
Bring to the boil and then simmer uncovered until the sauce is reduced to your desired thickness.
Season to taste and serve with thin slices of strudel.

Yellow Pepper Casserole in Beer

This is a rich warming winter dish which improves the longer and slower it cooks.

Serves 6

4 tablespoons olive oil

225gms shallots, peeled and cut into halves

4 medium aubergines, cut into 4 cm strips

4 garlic cloves, finely chopped

4 medium yellow peppers, sliced finely

275ml vegetable stock

500ml dark beer, such as Newcastle Brown

1 heaped teaspoon marmite or yeast extract

3 tablespoons apple juice concentrate

sea salt and freshly ground black pepper

4 medium potatoes, washed but not peeled

sunflower oil for frying the potatoes

175gms cheddar cheese, grated

Preheat the oven to 150C/Gas2/300F.
Heat the olive oil in a wok or large saucepan.
Add the shallots and sauté for a few minutes.
Add the aubergine strips, chopped garlic, sliced yellow peppers and stir fry for a few more minutes.
Spoon the stir fried vegetables into an oven-proof casserole dish with a well fitting lid.
Add the stock, beer, marmite and apple juice concentrate.

Stir well and season to taste.

Bring to the boil on top of the cooker and then place in the preheated oven for a long slow, cook, approximately 1½ hours.

In the meantime, parboil the potatoes with the skins on.

Drain, dry and slice them into thin rounds.

Fry the potatoes in sunflower oil until golden brown.

Drain on kitchen paper.

When the casserole is cooked, top with the fried potatoes and sprinkle with grated cheddar.

Return the casserole to the oven or under the grill until golden brown.

Serve in deep bowls with chunky slices of bread to mop up the juices.

Spicy Couscous Stuffed Cabbage Leaves

A light spicy dish served with a refreshing yoghurt, fresh coriander and mint sauce.

Serves 6

2 savoy cabbages

2 tablespoons olive oil

1 small onion, finely chopped

1 small red pepper, finely chopped

100gms mushrooms, finely chopped

50gms peas

1 large carrot, peeled and finely chopped

85gms broccoli, finely chopped

2 garlic cloves, finely chopped

110gms couscous, uncooked

½ teaspoon turmeric

1 teaspoon vegetable bouillon powder

250ml boiling water

1½ teaspoons hot pepper sauce

freshly ground black pepper

Sauce

500ml plain, thick and creamy yoghurt

2 tablespoons single cream

2 tablespoons fresh coriander, finely chopped

1 tablespoon fresh mint, finely chopped

1 teaspoon turmeric

1 teaspoon fresh lemon juice

3 teaspoons apple juice concentrate

Stuffed Cabbage Leaves

Preheat oven to 200C/Gas6/400F.

Remove as many large leaves from the cabbages as you can, aiming to have two large leaves per person.

Plunge them into boiling water for 1 minute.

Remove and drain.

Heat the olive oil in a wok or large saucepan.

Add the chopped onions and sauté until soft.

Add all the remaining prepared vegetables, including the garlic, and sauté until they are just beginning to soften.

In a large heat proof bowl mix the turmeric evenly into the dry couscous.

Mix the vegetable bouillon with boiling water and pour it over the couscous so that it is covered by approximately 2cms of liquid.

Leave the couscous for about 10 minutes to absorb the liquid and then fluff up with a fork.

Mix the stir fried vegetables with the hot pepper sauce, black pepper and the soaked couscous.

Spread out the blanched cabbage leaves and spoon a portion of the couscous mixture into each cabbage leaf.

Roll up each one into a neat parcel and place into an oven proof dish, seam side down.

Cover with silverfoil and bake in the preheated oven for 20-30 minutes.

Sauce

Mix the yoghurt and cream together and add the chopped herbs, turmeric, lemon juice and apple juice concentrate.

Serve the stuffed cabbage leaves hot with the sauce cold.

Oyster Mushroom and Leek Gougère

A gougère is made with savoury choux pastry and then filled with your choice of filling. Choux paste is easy to make, as long as you measure the ingredients out carefully and use a thick bottomed, high sided saucepan, preferably non-stick.

Serves 4

Choux Paste

50gms butter

150ml water

60gms unbleached white flour, sieved

2 free range eggs, beaten

75gms cheddar cheese, diced

½ teaspoon mustard powder

sea salt and freshly ground black pepper

1 tablespoon breadcrumbs

Filling

3 small leeks, washed and sliced

125gms oyster mushrooms

25gms butter

1 teaspoon shoyu

sea salt and freshly ground black pepper

Preheat the oven to 200C/Gas6/400F.
To make the choux paste, measure out the ingredients carefully.
Pour the water into a high sided saucepan and add the butter.
Bring the water and butter to the boil and immediately remove from the heat.
When the butter is melted, immediately add the sieved flour and beat with a wooden spoon until smooth and silky.
Allow to cool.
While the choux paste is cooling fry the sliced leeks in the butter, stirring well for a few minutes.
Add the oyster mushrooms.
Fry for a few more minutes and then add the shoyu and freshly ground black pepper.
Put to one side, whilst you finish the choux paste.
When the choux paste is cool, beat in the eggs a little at a time.
Add $^2/_3$ of the finely diced cheddar and season with the mustard powder, sea salt and freshly ground black pepper.
Fill a buttered oven-proof shallow dish with $^2/_3$ of the choux paste.
Dip your fingers in warm water and hollow out the centre.
Fill the hollow with the cooked mushrooms and leeks.
Partially cover with the remainder of the choux paste, leaving a gap around the edge of the dish.
Sprinkle the top with the remainder of the cheese and some brown bread crumbs.
Bake in the preheated oven for 30-40minutes or until the top is golden brown and the choux is well risen.
Serve at once.

Tempura Vegetables

This tempura batter is egg free and covers the vegetables with a thick, spicy coating.

Serves 8

Batter

300gms gram flour

50gms plain flour

2 teaspoons baking powder

2 teaspoons ground coriander

2 teaspoons ground cumin

2 teaspoons cayenne

2 teaspoons turmeric

2 teaspoons salt

300ml water

100ml lemon juice

1 tablespoon sunflower oil

1 tablespoon chopped fresh coriander

Vegetables

2 courgettes, sliced diagonally

2 carrots, peeled and sliced diagonally

1 head broccoli, cut into sprigs

1 red pepper, cut in thin strips

1 yellow pepper, cut in thin strips

sunflower oil, for deep frying

Shoyu Dip

2 tablespoons shoyu

4 tablespoons toasted sesame oil

1 teaspoon chilli sauce

1 teaspoon apple juice concentrate

Batter
Sieve the gram flour, plain flour and the baking powder into a large bowl.
Add the spices and the salt and mix well.
Slowly mix in the water, lemon juice and sunflower oil and whisk together to a smooth batter.
Stir in the chopped coriander.
Leave the batter to stand for 30 minutes.

Shoyu Dip
Make the shoyu dip by mixing all of the ingredients together.

Tempura
Heat the oil in a deep fryer or a wok.
Don't make it too hot, as this is a thick batter and needs a medium heat to cook through.
Coat the vegetables, a few at a time, with the batter and then place straight into the oil.
Fry them until they are crisp and golden.
Drain on kitchen paper to absorb any excess oil.
Eat at once dipping them in the shoyu dip.

Tropical Tofu Kebabs

You will need 12 wooden kebab sticks. Serve the kebabs with satay sauce.

Serves 6

Tofu

285gms plain tofu, cut into 24 cubes

Marinade

100ml shoyu

2 tablespoons toasted sesame oil

Vegetables

24 button mushrooms

1 large yellow pepper, cut into 24 Kebab sized chunks

1 large red pepper, cut into 24 Kebab sized chunks

2 small courgettes, cut into 24 rounds

1 avocado, peeled and cut into 24 cubes

1 small pineapple, cut into 24 cubes

Satay Sauce

1 green chilli, de-seeded

½ onion, peeled and chopped

2 garlic cloves, peeled

2cms of peeled fresh ginger root

450gms peanut butter

½ packet creamed coconut, chopped

juice of 1 large lemon

75ml shoyu

2 tablespoons brown sugar

150ml apple juice

Marinade

Mix the shoyu and the toasted sesame oil together in a bowl.
Marinate the tofu in the shoyu mixture for 1 hour, stirring
occasionally so that the tofu marinates evenly.
Whilst the tofu is marinating, make the satay sauce

Satay Sauce

The easiest way to make satay sauce is in a food processor.
Blend the chilli, onion, garlic and ginger to a fine pulp in the
food processor and then transfer this mixture to an oiled, thick
bottomed saucepan and fry for a few minutes.
Put the peanut butter, creamed coconut, lemon juice, shoyu,
brown sugar and apple juice into the food processor.
Blend to a smooth porridge like consistency, adding water if
necessary.
Add the peanut mixture to the onion mixture in the saucepan
and cook for a few minutes, stirring often.

Kebabs

Prepare the vegetables and fruit, cutting them into kebab sized
chunks that can be easily pushed onto the kebab sticks.
Drain the tofu, keeping the marinade for basting the kebabs.
Preheat the oven to 200C/Gas6/400F.
Now thread each kebab stick with a colourful combination of
two pieces of each type of vegetable, fruit and tofu.
Place the kebabs on a baking tray and baste them with the
left-over marinade.
Bake them in the preheated oven for 15 minutes, turning and
basting them twice.
Serve the kebabs at once with the satay sauce.

Thai Red Curry

For this recipe you will need some specialised ingredients.
Lemon grass, ideally fresh, but bottled will do.
Thai curry paste, available in oriental shops, (make sure that it is
vegetarian, because it often has added fish paste).
You will also need a tin of coconut milk and a packet of creamed
coconut, not to be confused with desiccated coconut.
Be warned, this curry is very, very, hot!

Serves 6

2 tablespoons toasted sesame oil

1 large onion, finely sliced

2 tablespoons Thai red curry paste

400gm tin of coconut milk

½ packet creamed coconut, dissolved in 500ml boiling water

2 garlic cloves, crushed

1 courgette, sliced

1 carrot, peeled and cut into thin strips

1 red pepper, cut into strips

1 potato, peeled and diced

4 mushrooms, sliced

3 tomatoes, quartered

1 green chilli, sliced finely, with the seeds removed

1 quill lemon grass

1 tablespoon lemon juice

1 tablespoon shoyu

Wash and prepare the vegetables.
Heat the toasted sesame oil in a large saucepan and fry the onion until soft and translucent.
Mix the Thai red curry paste with the coconut milk and add to the cooked onions.
Dissolve the creamed coconut in the boiling water and add to the onion mixture.
Add all the remaining ingredients and bring to the boil.
Simmer gently until the carrots and potatoes are just soft.
Remove the lemon grass quill before serving.
Serve on a bed of Thai scented rice.

Salads
&
Dressings

Celeriac and Haloumi Salad

Haloumi is a solid Greek cheese, similar to feta. Celeriac is a turnip shaped rooted variety of celery. The root is very knarled and ugly, but when you cut away the skin, the heart of the celeriac is creamy with the flavour of a mild celery.

Serves 6

250gms haloumi, cut into small cubes

1 medium celeriac root, peeled and grated

2 sticks of celery, and some of the leaf chopped

1 carrot, peeled and grated

Dressing

2 tablespoons olive oil

1 tablespoon lime juice

freshly ground black pepper

Fry the cubed haloumi in a dry frying pan, until golden.
This will take about 10 minutes.
Peel and grate the celeriac.
Submerge it in water with lemon juice squeezed into it, in order to stop the celeriac turning brown.
Chop the celery including the best of the green tops.
Peel and grate the carrot.
Mix the drained, grated celeriac with the grated carrot and the chopped celery.
Add the haloumi.
Prepare the dressing, pour over the salad and mix well.
Add lots of freshly ground pepper.

Chickpea and Red Pepper Salad

Serves 6

250gms chickpeas, dried weight or 2 x 425gm tins chickpeas.

2 medium red peppers, grilled and cut into strips

150gms french beans, blanched and cut into 2cm lengths

½ medium onion, sliced

1 tablespoon fresh coriander, chopped

Dressing

100ml sunflower oil

75ml wine vinegar

1 tablespoon tomato paste

1 small orange, juiced

sea salt and freshly ground black pepper

Soak the chickpeas overnight.
Drain, rinse and cook until tender.
If using tinned chickpeas, drain and rinse before use.
Cut the peppers in half, de-seed and place under a hot grill until the skin is blistered.
Cut into strips.
Blanch the french beans, plunge them into cold water to retain their colour and cut them into 2cm lengths.
Peel and slice the onion and chop the coriander.
Mix all the salad vegetables together with the cooked chickpeas.
Prepare the dressing, pour over the salad and mix in well.

Goats Cheese and Walnut Salad

Serves 4

2 cylindrical capricorn goats cheeses

8 slices granary bread

50gms walnuts

1 lollo rosso lettuce

Dressing

4 tablespoons walnut oil

2 tablespoons balsamic vinegar

freshly ground black pepper

Slice each goats cheese into 4 rounds.
With a round cutter a little bigger than the goats cheese, press
out 8 rounds of granary bread and place a round of goats
cheese on each round of granary bread.
Wash the lollo rosso lettuce and leave to drain.
Mix the dressing.
Grill the goats cheese rounds under a hot grill, until the cheese
begins to brown and bubble.
Decorate 4 medium sized plates with the lollo rosso lettuce and
place two rounds of goats cheese on each plate.
Sprinkle with walnuts, drizzle with the dressing and add lots of
freshly ground black pepper.
Serve at once.

Greek Style Salad

Serves 4

    1 packet feta cheese, cut into cubes

    4 tomatoes, cubed

    1 red onion, sliced into rings

    1 small green pepper, sliced

    1 small red pepper, sliced

    ½ cucumber, cubed

    100gms pitted black olives

    1 tablespoon fresh chopped oregano

    4 tablespoons olive oil

    freshly ground black pepper

In a salad bowl, mix the cubed feta cheese with the prepared salad vegetables.
Add the olives and the oregano and mix well.
Mix in the olive oil and add lots of freshly ground black pepper.
Serve at once with warm pitta bread.

Tricolour Pasta Salad

Serves 4

350gms spiral pasta, dried weight

4 tomatoes, cut in thin segments

½ onion, peeled and sliced

½ green pepper, grilled and then sliced

½ red pepper, grilled and then sliced

½ yellow pepper, grilled and then sliced

200gms sweetcorn, cooked

Dressing

150ml olive oil

75ml wine vinegar

30ml lemon juice

1 tablespoon tomato paste

25ml apple juice concentrate

2 garlic cloves, crushed

sea salt and freshly ground black pepper

Cook the pasta in lots of boiling salted water, until just tender.
Drain and rinse under cold water.
Prepare the salad vegetables, chopping them to same length as
the pasta spirals.
Mix the pasta and the chopped vegetables together in a salad
bowl.
Prepare the dressing, pour over the salad and mix well.

Pink Fir Apple Potato Salad

Fir apple potatoes are waxy with pink skins and a knobbly appearance.
This salad is served warm, but can be served cold with a vinaigrette or a
mayonnaise.

Serves 4

500gms pink fir apple potatoes

Dressing

2 tablespoons olive oil

1 tablespoon toasted sesame oil

½ tablespoon white wine vinegar

½ tablespoon lemon juice

1 teaspoon dijon mustard

1 teaspoon apple juice concentrate

Boil the potatoes with their skins on, until just tender.
Drain and keep warm.
Prepare the dressing and heat it in a small saucepan.
Slice the potatoes and place them into a serving dish.
Pour the hot dressing over the potatoes.
Briefly toss them in the dressing and serve at once.

Red Kidney Bean, Celery and Apple Salad

Serves 6

250gms red kidney beans, dried weight

or

2 x 425gm tins of unsweetened red kidney beans

4 celery sticks, washed and chopped into kidney bean sized pieces

2 large green peppers, sliced into strips

2 eating apples, washed, cored and chopped

½ onion, finely chopped

1 tablespoon chopped fresh basil

Dressing

100ml olive oil

75ml wine vinegar

1 tablespoon tomato puree

40ml fresh orange juice

2 teaspoons hot pepper sauce

sea salt and freshly ground black pepper

Soak the red kidney beans overnight.
Drain, rinse and cook them until tender.
If using tinned beans, drain and rinse before use.
Prepare the salad vegetables and mix them with the cooked kidney beans in a salad bowl.
Prepare the dressing and stir into the salad.

Stir Fry Salad

Serves 6

1 large carrot, peeled and cut into thin strips

2 medium courgettes, cut into thin strips

½ yellow pepper, cut into thin strips

½ red pepper, cut into thin strips

150gms bean sprouts

160gms french beans, blanched

150gms white cabbage, shredded

½ medium onion, finely sliced

20 gms fresh ginger root, peeled and grated

Dressing

100ml shoyu

2 tablespoons toasted sesame oil

1 tablespoon lemon juice

2 tablespoons apple juice concentrate

1 tablespoon wine vinegar

Prepare all the vegetables and mix together in a salad bowl.
Make the dressing and stir into the salad.
Chill the salad for 1 hour to let the vegetables marinate in the dressing.

Vegan Mayonnaise

This mayonnaise is egg-free and very easy to make.

135ml soya milk

1½ tablespoons cider vinegar

½ tablespoon lemon juice

1½ teaspoons whole grain mustard

300ml sunflower oil

sea salt and freshly ground black pepper

Place all the ingredients except the oil and the salt and pepper into a food processor.
Blend until well mixed.
In exactly the same way as making classic mayonnaise, trickle the oil in very slowly whilst the food processor is running.
The consistency of the mixture will gradually thicken as the oil is trickled in.
Finally add sea salt and freshly ground black pepper to taste.

French Vinaigrette

200ml virgin olive oil

or

100ml virgin olive oil and 100ml sunflower oil

50ml white wine vinegar

1 tablespoon lemon juice

2 teaspoons apple juice concentrate

3 teaspoons whole grain mustard

2 garlic cloves, peeled and crushed

sea salt and freshly ground black pepper

Either by hand or in a food processor, mix the oil, vinegar, lemon juice, apple juice concentrate, mustard and crushed garlic.
Blend or whisk until the vinaigrette takes on a creamy, silky appearance.
Add sea salt and freshly ground black pepper to taste.

Balsamic Vinaigrette

Balsamic vinegar is made from the juice of sweet Trebbiano grapes and then aged in wooden barrels.
It has a slightly sweet tangy taste and a rich dark colour.
The expense of balsamic vinegar makes extra virgin olive oil its only worthy partner

200ml extra virgin olive oil

50ml balsamic vinegar

1 tablespoon lemon juice

2 teaspoons apple juice concentrate

3 teaspoons whole grain mustard

2 garlic cloves, peeled and crushed

sea salt and freshly ground black pepper, to taste

Either by hand or in a food processor, mix the olive oil, balsamic vinegar, lemon juice, apple juice concentrate, mustard and crushed garlic.
Blend or whisk until the vinaigrette takes on a creamy silky appearance.
Add sea salt and freshly ground black pepper to taste.

Puddings

Apple and Fruit Crumble

You can use what ever fruits are in season, such as rhubarb in the spring, raspberries in the summer or pears in the autumn. Cooking apple is a good base for what ever more exotic fruit you choose, just make up the total weight of fruit to 1 kilo.

Serves 6

750gms cooking apples, peeled and cored

250gms pears, peeled and cored

50gms soft light brown sugar

½ teaspoon cinnamon

50ml apple juice

Topping

125gms sunflower margarine

150gms plain flour

50gms porridge oats

50gms jumbo oats

125gms soft light brown sugar

½ teaspoon nutmeg

Preheat the oven to 190C/Gas5/375F.
Cut the apples and the pears into bite sized chunks.
Place them in a thick bottomed saucepan with the cinnamon, sugar and apple juice and simmer until the apples are soft.

Topping
Rub the margarine into the flour in a large bowl until it resembles bread crumbs.
Add the oats, sugar and nutmeg and mix well.
Place the cooked fruit mixture into an oven-proof dish, cover with the topping and cook in the preheated oven for 30 minutes or until the crumble is golden brown.

Banoffi Pie

Banoffi pie is the most popular pudding at Demuths because of its totally over the top calorific content.

Serves 6

Biscuit Base

125gms butter, melted

225gms digestive biscuits

Banoffi Topping

125gms butter

100gms caster sugar

400gms can of sweetened condensed milk

4 bananas

300ml whipping cream

Crush the biscuits in a plastic bag until they have the consistency of breadcrumbs.
Mix them with the melted butter and press into a 25cm loose bottomed shallow cake tin, evenly covering the bottom.
Chill in the fridge.

Topping
Place the butter and sugar in a bain-marie over a medium heat.
Stir until the sugar has melted into the butter and there are no sugar granules left.
Add the condensed milk and stir until the mixture starts to come away from the sides and is the colour of caramel (about 30mins).
Pour the toffee mixture onto the prepared biscuit case and chill again until the toffee is set.
When really cold, cover with sliced bananas and top with whipped cream.

Bramley Apple Sponge

A lovely moist apple sponge with a crunchy topping. The sweetness of the sponge is offset by the tartness of the Bramley apples.

Serves 6

1 bramley apple thinly sliced, but not peeled

2 free range eggs

250gms caster sugar

150ml single cream, or creamy milk

110gms butter

185gms white self raising flour, sieved

demerara sugar, to sprinkle on top

Preheat the oven to 200C/Gas6/400F.
Grease and line with baking parchment a shallow 20cm cake tin.
Wash, core and thinly slice the bramley apple into segments.
Whisk the eggs and the sugar together until pale and creamy.
In a saucepan heat the cream, or creamy milk, with the butter until the mixture comes to the boil.
Allow to cool to blood temperature and then stir the warm cream mixture into the egg and sugar mixture.
Fold in the sifted white self raising flour.
Layer the cake batter and apples alternatively, starting and ending with a layer of cake batter.
Sprinkle the top with a little demerara sugar.
Bake in the middle of the preheated oven for 30 minutes until golden and springy to the touch.
Serve warm with lashings of cream.

Apricot and Almond Daquoise

These almond meringues are served with whipped cream and
apricot puree. The meringues can be made in advance and kept
in a sealed tin.

Serves 6

- 3 egg whites
- 175gms caster sugar
- 75gms ground almonds
- 175gms dried apricots
- 1 lemon, juiced
- 75gms toasted flaked almonds
- 150ml whipping cream

Preheat the oven to 150C/Gas2/300F.
Whisk the egg whites until just stiff and peaked.
Add 2 heaped tablespoons of the caster sugar and whisk until
the meringue mixture looks shiny.
Fold in the remaining sugar with the ground almonds.
Grease a baking sheet and line with baking parchment.
Grease the baking parchment as well, to make certain that the
meringues do not stick.
Dollop the meringue mixture onto the prepared baking sheet in
individual circles, approximately 10cm in diameter, leaving a
5cm gap between each meringue.
Place on the middle shelf of the preheated oven.
Bake for 1½ hours or until the meringues have dried out.

While the meringues are baking, soak the apricots in boiling water until soft and plump.
Drain the apricots and blend in a food processor with the lemon juice to a thick purée.
Toast the almonds under a hot grill and whip the cream.
To serve place one meringue in the centre of a dessert plate and half cover with whipped cream, then add a dollop of apricot puree and sprinkle with toasted almonds.

Calvados and Apple Pudding with Almond Meringue

A winter pudding, with the calvados giving the apples a lovely warming fieriness.

Serves 6

1300gms bramley apples, peeled, cored & thickly sliced

1 lemon, zest and juice

100ml water

225gms caster sugar

3 tablespoons calvados

3 egg whites

50gms ground almonds

½ teaspoon cinnamon

½ teaspoon nutmeg

Preheat the oven 150C/Gas2/300F.
Put the apples, the lemon zest and juice, the water and half of the sugar into a thick bottomed saucepan.
Cook for approximately 15 minutes over a low heat, stirring frequently until the apples are soft and mushy.
Remove from the heat and stir in the calvados.
Whisk the egg whites until stiff and peaked.
Next, gradually add the remaining sugar, whisking all the time.
Finally, fold in the ground almonds.
Place the apple mixture into a greased oven proof dish and then spread the meringue mixture evenly over the top.
Bake in the preheated oven for approximately 30 minutes or until the meringue is crisp.
Take out of the oven sprinkle the top with a mixture of cinnamon and nutmeg and serve at once.

Chestnut, Orange and Chocolate Slice

A wonderfully rich vegan pudding to serve at Christmas time.

Serves 6

1 tablespoon sunflower oil

225gms vegan dark chocolate

175gms sunflower margarine

175gms caster sugar

425gms tin of unsweetened chestnut puree

2 oranges, zest and juice

Line the base and short sides of a 450gms loaf tin with a strip of greaseproof paper long enough to hang over at the ends. Oil the lined tin well with sunflower oil.
Break the chocolate into pieces and melt in a bain-marie or in the microwave on the 'defrost' setting.
Beat the margarine and sugar together until pale and creamy. Next, beat in the chestnut puree and the zest and juice of the oranges.
Add the melted chocolate & stir in.
The mixture should be smooth and custard like.
Spoon the mixture into the prepared tin and smooth the top with a palette knife.
Chill for at least 10 hours in the refrigerator, or until set.
To serve, slide a palette knife around the edges of the tin and use the overhanging pieces of greaseproof paper to lift the slice out of the tin.
Turn out onto a serving dish and peel off the greaseproof.
Slice thinly and serve cold with vegan soya cream.

Chocolate Fudge Cake

Vegans usually get a raw deal when it comes to cakes and puddings requiring eggs to make them rise. This is an exception. This cake can be iced or served warm as a pudding with hot chocolate sauce.

Serves 8

Cake

300gms self raising flour

3 teaspoons baking powder

50gms cocoa

250gms caster sugar

1 teaspoon pure vanilla essence

9 tablespoons sunflower oil

175ml orange juice

175ml water

Topping

250gms icing sugar

1 tablespoon cocoa

50gms vegan sunflower margarine

3 tablespoons boiling water

Cake
Preheat the oven to 190C/Gas5/375F.
Grease and line a 20cm cake tin with baking parchment.
Sift the flour, baking powder and cocoa into a large mixing bowl.

Add the caster sugar, vanilla essence, sunflower oil, orange juice and water.
Whisk to a batter like consistency.
Pour into the prepared tin.
Bake in the middle of the preheated oven for approximately 40 minutes or until a skewer when inserted in the cake comes out clean.

Topping
Sift the icing sugar and the cocoa into a bowl.
Melt the margarine with the boiling water.
Add the margarine mixture to the sugar mixture and mix well.
The sauce will harden as it cools.
As a sauce, serve hot.
As an icing, spread the warm topping over the cake and leave to harden.

Strawberry Baked Cheesecake

This recipe makes a large cheesecake, ideal for a summer party.
Decorate it with fresh strawberries.

Serves 10

225gms digestive biscuits, crushed into crumbs

110gms butter, melted

600gms cream cheese

5 free range eggs

200gms caster sugar

1 teaspoon pure vanilla essence

225gms fresh strawberries

275ml whipping cream

Preheat the oven to 170C/Gas3/325F.
Crush the digestive biscuits in a plastic bag to a breadcrumb
consistency.
Mix them with the melted butter.
Press the biscuit mixture into a 25cm loose bottomed flan tin to
form a base for the cheesecake mixture.
Leave to harden.
Blend the cream cheese, eggs, caster sugar and vanilla essence
together in a food processor.
Pour the mixture over the biscuit base and place in the
preheated oven on a baking sheet.
Cook for 40 minutes or until set and pale golden in colour.
Leave to cool overnight and chill before serving.
Just before serving, top the cheesecake with whipped cream
and fresh strawberries.

Hunza Cream

Hunza apricots or wild apricots are grown in the Himalayas. These apricots are small and fawn in colour and have a sweet nutty flavour. You can buy them in most wholefood shops.

Serves 6

250gms hunza apricots

500gms greek strained yoghurt

1 tablespoon caster sugar

zest of 1 lemon

juice of ½ lemon

Soak the apricots in boiling water for a couple of hours.
Put the soaked apricots into a saucepan with the juice that they were soaking in and bring to the boil.
Simmer with a lid on for 20 minutes.
Leave to cool and then remove the stones from the apricots.
Liquidize the apricot flesh with enough of the cooking juice to make a smooth, thick purée.
Mix in the yoghurt, lemon zest, lemon juice and sweeten with sugar to taste.
Chill before serving.

Cinnamon Pears

This is a very easy dessert to make when you have a glut of pears. It is best made the day before to give the spices time to infuse into the pears. Serve hot or cold.

Serves 6

800gms pears

550ml unsweetened apple juice

75ml apple juice concentrate

1 piece fresh ginger root, 2 cms long

1 teaspoon cinnamon

Preheat the oven to 200C/Gas6/400F.
Slice the washed cored unpeeled pears into thin wedges.
Spread the sliced pears evenly into a deep baking dish.
Mix the cinnamon into the apple juice.
Pour the apple juice and the apple concentrate over the pears.
Grate the ginger with the skin still on, using a fine grater.
Take the grated ginger into the palm of your hand and squeeze the ginger juice over the pears.
Cook the pears on the top shelf of the preheated oven until soft.
Serve hot or cold.

Dark Chocolate Mousse

This mousse is deliciously simple. It requires the best possible dark chocolate.

Serves 4

200gms dark chocolate

5 free range eggs

1 teaspoon pure vanilla essence

Melt the chocolate in a bain-marie or on the 'defrost' setting of a microwave.
Leave it to cool slightly.
Separate the eggs.
Whisk the whites to the consistency of stiff peaks.
Beat the egg yolks and then mix them with the melted chocolate and vanilla essence.
Fold the egg whites into the chocolate mixture ensuring it is mixed in really well.
Pour into a serving dish or individual ramekins.
Leave to cool and set in the refrigerator overnight.
Decorate with whipped cream.

Fresh Fruit Pavlova

This meringue is a summer favourite, filled with seasonal fruit, whipped cream and yoghurt. The addition of the yoghurt cuts through the richness of this dessert and gives it a lighter quality.

Serves 6

3 free range egg whites

185gms caster sugar

½ teaspoon pure vanilla essence

250ml whipping cream

100ml plain yoghurt

350gms seasonal fruits

Preheat the oven to 140C/Gas1/275F.
Line a lightly oiled baking sheet with baking parchment.
Whisk the egg whites until they form soft peaks.
Add the sugar a little at a time, whisking it briskly after each addition until all the sugar has been added.
Next fold in the vanilla essence.
With a large metal spoon, dollop half the meringue mixture onto the prepared baking tray, to make a 20cm round.
Using the other half, dollop small blobs adjoining each other to form a circle around the edge of the meringue round.
Leave an indentation in the middle for the filling.
Place the meringue in the preheated oven and cook for 1½ hours.
If the meringue starts to turn yellow the oven is too hot.

PUDDINGS

The secret of a lily-white meringue is long, slow cooking.
When cooked, turn off the oven and leave the meringue in
place overnight to dry out.
The next day whip the cream and mix in the yoghurt.
(It's important that the cream is stiffly beaten as the addition of
the yoghurt will make the mixture more sloppy.)
To serve, fill the centre of the meringue with the whipped cream
and yoghurt mixture.
Pile the seasonal fruits on top.
Serve immediately.

Spiced Apricot Compôte with Port and Juniper Berries

We serve this compôte at Christmas as a vegan, gluten-free alternative to Christmas Pudding.

Serves 6

450gms dried unsulphured apricots

50gms sultanas

300ml unsweetened apple juice

100ml water

1 level teaspoon ground cinnamon

1 level teaspoon ground nutmeg

2 teaspoons juniper berries

2 tablespoons apple juice concentrate

4 tablespoons port

Place all of the ingredients, except the port, into a heavy bottomed saucepan and bring to the boil.
Turn down the heat and simmer gently until the apricots are soft, approximately 30 minutes.
Add the port and continue to simmer for 5 minutes, adding more water if the mixture is too thick.
Serve hot or cold.

Raspberry and Apricot Parfait

This parfait is very light, best served in individual dishes as the raspberry and apricot purées are swirled together.

Serves 6

2 egg whites

125gms caster sugar

275ml whipping cream

125gms fresh or frozen raspberries

275gms tinned unsweetened apricot halves

Whisk the egg whites to form soft peaks.
Whisk the caster sugar into the egg whites a little at a time.
Whip the cream until it is stiff.
Fold the whipped cream into the egg white mixture.
In a food processor, blend the raspberries and apricots separately, with a little juice, to make smooth purées.
Divide the egg white and whipped cream mixture into two.
Stir the puréed raspberries into one half and the puréed apricots into the other.
Place a spoon full of each mixture into individual serving bowls and swirl together.
Chill before serving.

Hot Lemon Syrup Sponge

This sponge is tangy and oozing with syrup. Best eaten warm with lashings of cream.

Serves 6

Sponge

225gms sunflower margarine

225gms caster sugar

225gms unbleached white flour

3 teaspoons baking powder

4 free range eggs

1½ lemons, zest and juice

Lemon Syrup

70ml lemon juice

50ml golden syrup

150ml boiling water

Preheat the oven to 200C/Gas6/400F.
Grease and line a 25cm loose bottomed, low sided cake tin with baking parchment.
In a large mixing bowl, whisk the sunflower margarine and the sugar until pale and creamy.
Sieve the flour and the baking powder into another bowl.
Slowly whisk one egg at a time into the creamy margarine mixture, adding a little sieved flour to stop the eggs curdling.
When all the eggs are mixed in, add the lemon juice and zest.
Finally fold in the remaining flour.
The mix should be sloppy.

Pour the sponge mix into the prepared tin.
Bake in the centre of the preheated oven for approximately
40 minutes or until golden in colour and spongy to the touch.
While the sponge is cooling make the lemon syrup.
Mix the lemon juice, golden syrup and boiling
water together in a jug to make a smooth sauce.
With a skewer, prick the top of the sponge all over.
Pour the sauce over the sponge allowing it to soak in through
the holes.
Serve at once.

Iced Cream Ginger Meringue with a Raspberry Coulis

The quantities for this pudding are large, because it is kept in the freezer and you can cut off a slice or two whenever you need an instant pudding.

Serves 10

Meringue

4 egg whites

200gms soft brown sugar

1 teaspoon ground ginger

10 tablespoons whipping cream

500ml thick natural yoghurt

4 teaspoons orange juice

4 teaspoons orange zest

Coulis

250gms fresh or frozen unsweetened raspberries

2 tablespoons soft brown sugar

250ml water

fresh mint leaves, for decoration

Meringue
Preheat the oven to 140C/Gas1/275F.
Grease a baking sheet, cover with baking parchment and then grease the baking parchment.
Whisk the egg whites until just stiff, then add half the sugar and the ground ginger and whisk again until the mixture is stiff and glossy.

Carefully fold in the remaining sugar with a metal spoon.
Spoon the meringue mixture onto the prepared baking sheet
and spread flat.
Cook in the preheated oven for approximately 1½ hours or until
dry.
When the meringue is cool, break into small pieces.
Whip the cream until thick.
Add the yoghurt and stir in the orange juice and zest.
Mix the crushed meringue pieces into the cream mixture.
Line a large loaf tin with baking parchment and pour in the
cream and meringue mixture.
Freeze until set for at least 4 hours.

Raspberry Coulis
Place the raspberries, sugar and water in a small saucepan
and bring to the boil.
Gently simmer for 10 minutes.
Strain the coulis through a fine sieve and leave it to cool

Serving
Remove the iced meringue from the freezer 10 minutes before
serving.
Slice the iced meringue with a sharp knife into the required
number of servings.
Place each slice of iced meringue onto a pool of raspberry
coulis.
Decorate with fresh mint leaves.

'Tarte Tatin'
Caramelised Apple Tart

This tart is made upside down with the pastry on the top and the apples on the bottom and then served the right way up with the caramelised apples oozing into the pastry.

Serves 8

Pastry

175gms unbleached white flour

75gms unsalted butter

2 tablespoons crème frâiche

Filling

25gms unsalted butter

110gms soft light brown sugar

1 level teaspoon cinnamon

400gms bramley apples

400gms granny smith apples

To make the pastry, rub the butter into the flour until it resembles breadcrumbs.
Add the crème frâiche and mix to a soft dough.
If you don't have crème frâiche, double cream is almost as good.
The addition of the crème frâiche makes the pastry sticky and difficult to handle, so touch it as little as possible.
Don't be tempted to add more flour, because the test of a good 'Tarte Tatin' is its melt in the mouth pastry.

The pastry will need at least one hour in the fridge to rest before you roll it out.

Preheat the oven to 200C/Gas6/400F.

Grease a 20cm loose bottomed flan dish.

Line it with baking parchment and then butter it copiously.

Mix together the sugar and cinnamon and sprinkle it over the bottom of the flan dish.

Peel, core and thinly slice the apples.

Mix the two types of apple together and arrange the slices in a circular pattern on top of the sugar.

Roll out the pastry to approximately 2cm thick and cut out a round to fit the flan dish.

Press the pastry gently over the apples tucking it down the inside of the dish.

Bake in the preheated oven for 40-50 minutes until the pastry is golden.

Leave to cool completely before attempting to turn it out.

When cold, loosen around the edges of the dish, place a large plate on top of the tart and turn the tart upside down.

Remove the dish and carefully peel off the baking parchment to reveal the caramelised apples.

Serve cold with lashings of crème frâiche or whipped cream.

Allessandro's Torta di Ricotta

This recipe comes from an Italian friend who cooked at the restaurant the first summer that we were open. It has a biscuity base and topping with a luscious ricotta and dark chocolate filling. Serve warm as a dessert or cold in small slices with coffee.

Serves 6

275gms unbleached white flour

½ teaspoon baking powder

80gms butter

120gms demerara sugar

1 small free range egg

275gms ricotta cheese

100gms caster sugar

150gms dark chocolate

milk, enough to make the ricotta mixture smooth and pourable

Preheat the oven to 200C/Gas6/400F.
Line a shallow greased flan tin with baking parchment.
To make the base and the topping of the tart, sieve the flour and the baking powder into a large mixing bowl.
Rub the butter into the flour until the mixture resembles breadcrumbs.
Add the sugar and mix in.
Lastly, add the beaten egg a little at a time, mixing to a crumbly pastry, too dry to roll out, but moist enough to press into the prepared tin.
Divide the crumble mixture into two.

Press half into the base of the prepared flan tin, reserving the other half for the topping.

To make the filling, crumble the ricotta into a mixing bowl and mix in the caster sugar.
Chop the chocolate into small chunks and add to the ricotta mixture.
Add sufficient milk to make the mixture sloppy and just pourable.
Pour the ricotta mixture onto the crumble base and sprinkle the remaining crumble mixture on top, so that all the ricotta mixture is covered.
Bake on the middle shelf of the preheated oven, for approximately 30 minutes until golden.
Cut into slices, whilst still warm & enjoy.

INDEX